EQUITY INDEXED ANNUITIES

Thomas F. Streiff, CFP, CLU, ChFC, CFS
Cynthia A. DiBiase, CFS

DEARBORN™
A **Kaplan Professional** Company

This publication is designed to provide accurate and authoritative information in regard to the subject matter covered. It is sold with the understanding that the publisher is not engaged in rendering legal, accounting or other professional service. If legal advice or other expert assistance is required, the services of a competent professional person should be sought.

This text is updated periodically to reflect changes in laws and regulations. To verify that you have the most recent update, you may call Dearborn at 1-800-423-4723.

©1999 by Dearborn Financial Publishing, Inc.®
Published by Dearborn Financial Institute, Inc.®

Printed in the United States of America.

First printing, March 1999

Library of Congress Cataloging-in-Publication Data

Streiff, Thomas F., 1958–
    Equity indexed annuities / Thomas F. Streiff, Cynthia A. DiBiase.
        p.   cm.
    ISBN 0–7931–2845–5
    1. Equity indexed annuities.   I. DiBiase, Cynthia A., 1958–
II. Title.
HG8790.5.S77   1999
332.024' 01– –dc21
                                    99–10247
                                        CIP

██████ Table of Contents

CHAPTER 8
PRODUCT DUE DILIGENCE

┅┅ About the Authors

Thomas F. Streiff, CFP, CLU, ChFC, CFS, is president and CEO of Talbot Financial Services and chairman and cofounder of NFC Consulting Group. Talbot Financial Services is a leading distributor of annuities and mutual funds through banks, broker-dealers and brokerage agencies. NFC is a financial services consulting firm specializing in annuity product design and distribution strategy, marketing research, continuing education and marketing consulting.

Streiff has earned a reputation nationwide as an expert on annuities and retirement planning. He has designed retirement products for insurance companies, mutual fund companies and financial institutions and has provided training and education for thousands of tax attorneys, accountants and other financial services professionals. A sought-after speaker, he has addressed national conferences for the AICPA and the National Endowment for Financial Education. He is a respected spokesperson for the annuity industry and has appeared before the federal government's General Accounting Office and the Securities and Exchange Commission to offer his opinions on various annuity topics. He serves as an advisory member of the American Council of Life Insurance's subcommittee on equity indexed annuities.

This is Streiff's third book for Dearborn Financial Publishing. He is the co-author of *Annuities* and *Distributions from Qualified Plans*, both of which are now in their second editions.

Cynthia A. DiBiase, CFS, is president and CEO of NFC Consulting Group. An expert on annuities and annuity product designs, she has developed fixed, variable and equity indexed annuity products and marketing strategies for insurers, mutual fund companies and financial institutions nationwide. She is a frequent speaker at financial services conferences and has addressed the Society of Actuaries, the Financial Institutions Insurance Association, the National Association of Insurance Commissioners and the National Association for Variable Annuities. She is an advisory member of the American Council of Life Insurance's subcommittee on equity indexed annuities and co-author of the industry's "Buyer's Guide" for the product.

DiBiase has led numerous training and educational seminars for financial services professionals across the country. She helped create NFC's "Annuity Information Center," which provides the industry with customized marketing research, and was also responsible for the development of IPOD™ (Index Products on Disk), an interactive software program containing educational and statistical data on equity indexed annuities.

▪▪▪▪▪ Introduction

I t has been quite some time since there has been a truly unique product innovation in the insurance industry. That changed in 1994 with the introduction of the first "modern" equity indexed annuity. Since that time, the market has expanded tremendously.

As the authors of this text traveled throughout the country for numerous speaking engagements and consulting assignments, they encountered life insurance agents, registered representatives and financial planners who had a real need for solid, unbiased education about equity indexed annuities. Rarely has there been so much interest in a single financial product. Nor has there been so much press—good and bad—disseminated about a single financial product. With this much interest and this much press, it's no wonder that there has been a lot of confusion and misinformation regarding equity indexed annuities. It is the authors' intent to set the record straight.

This text was written with the needs of different types of practitioners in mind. For those who are experienced annuity producers, the book offers an orientation to how EIAs contrast with other financial products with which they are already familiar. It delves into the mechanics and methodology of the equity indexed annuity to provide an in-depth look at what these products are all about, how they are designed, how they operate and how they might fit into a client's long-term retirement plans. For the practitioner who may be new to the world of annuities, this text offers a solid foundation on annuities in general—their purpose and function—so the remainder of the book and the information provided builds from there. Finally, for the practitioner who is not licensed to sell securities (and a securities license is not required for the vast majority of EIAs) the text provides guidance with respect to understanding, positioning and presenting these unique products to clients in an appropriate manner.

The equity indexed annuity represents a unique planning opportunity for today's consumers. However, it requires an educated and knowledgeable practitioner to embrace and communicate its distinct features and benefits. It is the authors' hope that this text will be read and referenced often by practitioners who are committed to expanded knowledge and good market conduct when dealing with clients and prospects.

Once the reader has become familiar with equity indexed annuities, he or she is encouraged to seek out additional means of staying current with this dynamic marketplace. Educational software marketed under the trade name IPOD™ (Index Products on Disk) was created by the authors of this text and is available through NFC Consulting Group, Chicago, Illinois.

1

Introduction to Equity Indexed Annuities

T he annuity has long been a staple of the retirement planner's portfolio. For years, practitioners have extolled the merits of fixed and variable annuities as long-term savings and retirement vehicles. Yet the message had begun to grow somewhat dated. Within these two categories of annuity products, there have been only slight variations in product design and functionality over the years—that is, until now. A truly unique addition to the annuity arena has arrived on the scene—the *equity indexed annuity*.

Equity indexed annuities, or EIAs as they are often called, represent a real departure from the design of all other annuities. These unique products provide the financial practitioner—and his or her clients—with opportunities that were not available in the past. However, along with these opportunities comes a responsibility. The responsibility is to take the time to learn and understand the nature of the equity indexed annuity and know how and when it is a suitable option for a client. The financial services professional needs some appropriate background information in order to explain EIAs to prospects and clients and help them make informed investment decisions. In this chapter, we will start down that road by taking a brief look at EIAs, their history and how they have evolved.

■ ■ ■ ■ ■

■ WHAT IS AN EQUITY INDEXED ANNUITY?

The best way to describe an equity indexed annuity is to compare it to something the practitioner is already familiar with—the traditional fixed deferred annuity. This is an easy comparison to make, not because the EIA compares well to a fixed deferred annuity, but because an EIA *is* a fixed deferred annuity.

An equity indexed annuity has all of the same features and guarantee-of-principal attributes of a fixed deferred annuity. The main difference is how the product's interest is credited. With a traditional fixed annuity, the interest rate credited to the contract is usually based on prevailing market rates. It is determined and declared in advance by the insurance company and is guaranteed payable for the subsequent

ILL. 1.1 ■ *Stock Market History Since 1970*

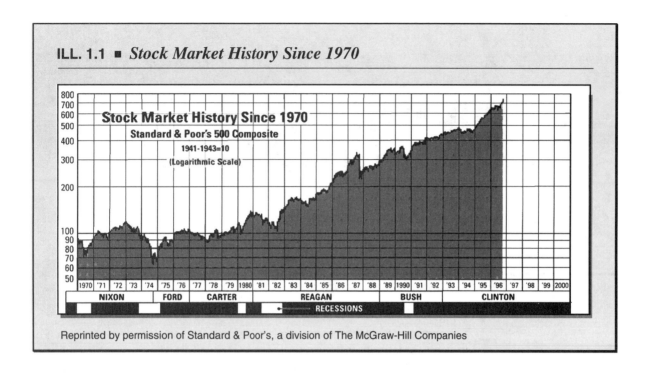

term of the contract—typically, one year. For each succeeding contract year, the same approach is used. For example, an insurer may declare that it will credit an interest rate of 8 percent upon the issuance of an annuity contract; that rate is guaranteed for the first year. Upon the anniversary of the issue date, a new interest rate is declared. It may again be 8 percent or it may be higher or lower, but it too is guaranteed payable for the next year. Underlying the contract for its life is a guaranteed minimum interest rate, usually 3 percent or 4 percent. The declared interest rate for any contract year is never less than the minimum rate.

With an EIA, the interest rate credited to the contract is not determined each year by the insurer. Instead, it is based on an interest-crediting formula that is linked to an independent stock market index. This, in a nutshell, is an EIA's defining characteristic. Therefore, an equity indexed annuity can be described as a "fixed deferred annuity that earns interest at a rate which is linked to an external stock market index." The index to which most EIAs on the market today tie their interest rates is the Standard & Poor's Composite Stock Price Index (the S&P 500), which is considered a significant barometer of the performance of U.S. equity markets.

It should be emphasized that an EIA is *not* an investment in the stock market, *not* a variable annuity and *not* a security or indexed mutual fund. Nor is an EIA a substitute for any of these products. First and foremost, it is a fixed annuity. A fixed annuity protects the owner from market risk; conservation of principal is guaranteed. When people speak of the safety of fixed annuities, this is usually what they're referring to. In essence, fixed annuities are used for the investment of "safe money" which will not be accessed for a number of years. Safe money is typically invested in financial products that have no risk to principal but—as a trade-off—usually offer a relatively low rate of return. Countering this trade-off is where the unique feature of the equity indexed annuity applies. An EIA provides an opportunity to achieve potentially greater growth and inflation protection, without market risk to principal. In this way, it adds a new and welcome dimension to "safe money" savings options. In addition, like all annuities, the EIA can be used to provide its owner a stream of income that is guaranteed to last as long as he or she lives. This income is typically used in retirement to supplement other sources of income such as personal savings, Social Security and pension benefits.

■ THE POPULARITY OF EIAs

Why did equity indexed annuities become so popular? To answer this question, we must look at the financial environment in recent years. Interest rates and the stock market are two of the driving forces that have fueled the development—and the popularity—of equity indexed annuities.

Throughout the mid- to late-1990s, interest rates (as represented by 10-year Treasury notes) were generally declining whereas the stock market was booming. During the period 1991 through 1998, for example, the stock market as measured by the S&P 500 Index averaged a 17.9 percent return. In contrast, yields on 10-year Treasury notes during this same time period ranged from a high of 8.28 percent to a low of 4.53 percent.

When market rates fall, rates on newly issued declared-rate fixed annuities will also fall. This is because the premium deposits of fixed annuity owners are part of the general account assets of the insurer and general account assets—which are used to fund the insurer's guaranteed products—are typically invested in fixed-interest rate instruments like corporate bonds or mortgages. If the interest rates on these vehicles decline, the insurer—which is now earning a lower rate of return on its investments—is likely to follow suit and credit a lower interest rate on its fixed annuity offerings.

In addition to falling interest rates and a booming stock market, there was another important reason why equity indexed annuities became popular. Now, as always, there is strong consumer interest in retirement products that offer safety of principal. Consumer surveys have indicated that many people consider safety of principal a primary factor when purchasing or investing in a particular retirement savings product. They rank safety of principal ahead of earnings potential, tax ramifications and inflation fears. Fixed annuities—indexed or not—provide this important feature.

Because the equity indexed annuity provides interest linked to a stock market index, yet protects against market risk, it bridges a major gap between traditional "safe money" vehicles—CDs, savings accounts and declared-rate fixed annuities—and riskier investment alternatives such as stocks and mutual funds. It provides another dimension to the ever-present needs for long-term accumulation and asset security.

A logical question that may come to mind is, "What about the future of EIAs in a declining or volatile stock market environment—will they remain popular?" As later chapters will point out, EIAs offer consumers some unique benefits *in all types of market environments*. One should not underestimate their value as a safe money alternative that provides the means to diversify such assets.

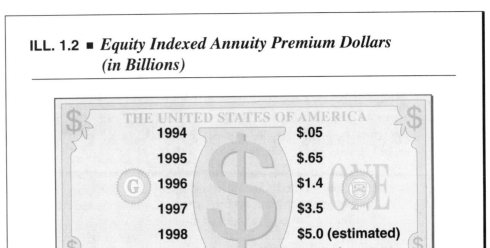

ILL. 1.2 ■ *Equity Indexed Annuity Premium Dollars (in Billions)*

1994	$.05
1995	$.65
1996	$1.4
1997	$3.5
1998	$5.0 (estimated)

■ THE EVOLUTION OF EIAs

The evolution of the equity indexed annuity began in the late 1980s. During this time, an equity indexed annuity was introduced by Fidelity Banker's Life. Neither the company nor the product exists today. In 1991, another much more successful product was introduced by National Home Life Insurance Company (now called Peoples Benefit Life, part of the AEGON USA group of life insurance companies). National Home Life offered an equity indexed general account option in its variable annuity. We consider this product to be the start of the modern era of equity indexed annuities.

The market for equity indexed annuities expanded greatly in 1994 and 1995 when Keyport Life and Lincoln Benefit Life introduced equity indexed annuities. Suddenly, sales of EIAs soared from millions of dollars to billions of dollars in new premium deposits.

Through 1998, many new EIA products entered the market. Today, there are more than 70 different product variations from 40 different companies. In 1997, equity indexed annuity sales accounted for more than 9 percent of fixed annuity sales— quite an accomplishment for a product that has been on the scene only a few short years. Some forecasts predict that by the year 2000, this market will grow to more than 100 products, representing tens of billions of premium dollars.

One might wonder why so many different indexed annuity product variations exist. The main reason is that there are a variety of methods that insurers use to measure changes in the index to which the EIAs' interest rates are linked—and each method equates to a different product variation. The EIA product also entails several features and "moving parts" that easily lend to customization and differentiation for specific distribution channels or markets. In this way, the insurance industry is quite creative. It has never shied away from designing distinctive products to serve the needs of targeted groups or individuals. The quest for product differentiation is the hallmark of any thriving, competitive industry; the equity indexed annuity is a prime example of this. This will become clear as we delve into the mechanics of EIAs in Chapters 3 and 4.

■ THE CONCEPT OF INDEXING

As a financial concept, indexing is not new. It has long been used as a way to measure or assess the behavior of the economy and markets within the economy. For example, the Consumer Price Index—an index with which most people are familiar—measures changes in the prices of goods and services. These changes, in turn, are indicators of inflation. The Dow Jones Industrial Average, which comprises 30 high quality blue-chip stocks and reflects their average price behavior, is thought to reflect overall stock market activity. Another index, noted earlier, is the Standard & Poor's 500 Index, which measures changes in the stock prices of 500 different companies that are leaders in their industries. In this context, the term "index" refers to a weighted average: it reflects the collective performance (based on average price per share) of the stocks that compose the index. Changes in the index, up or down, reflect the price behavior of the stock market in general.

It did not take long for financial products to incorporate the concept of indexing. In 1976, the Vanguard Group introduced the first mutual fund designed to mirror the S&P 500 by investing in stocks that make up the S&P 500. Many other funds have since followed suit, as have bank and insurance company financial products. In the late 1980s, for example, a number of financial institutions began to offer equity-linked CDs, tying their interest rates to the performance of the S&P 500.

The Popularity of Indexing

There are several reasons why indexing is so popular. With mutual funds, for example, there have been few investment managers whose funds have consistently outperformed or even met the market each year. Consequently, the indexed mutual fund was created and designed to mirror the performance of one of the major stock indexes, such as the S&P 500. It does so by purchasing stocks that make up the particular index. In this way, the return an investor receives on his or her mutual fund investment replicates the performance of the stock market index. Investing in an indexed product is a good way to obtain exposure to a wide range of individual securities and achieve diversification. In addition, indexing is an unmanaged approach to investing and, therefore, the costs are lower than an actively managed methodology. "Unmanaged" simply means that the asset manager need not employ the necessary resources to research and select appropriate assets for the fund because the assets are already identified as those being in the index. Many pension fund managers have utilized indexing as a low-cost means of diversifying assets. Using the contributions made to the plan, they simply purchase the same stocks (in the same proportions) that compose the index.

In addition to low costs and diversification, a financial product with returns linked to a stock market index like the S&P 500 also provides a hedge against inflation. Studies have shown that over long periods of time, the stock market has outperformed not only the inflation rate but also all other types of investments.

Indexing and the Annuity

The equity indexed annuity is just another application for an already popular and proven concept. It is important to note, however, that indexed annuities are significantly different than indexed mutual funds. Indexed mutual funds still carry market risk; there is risk of loss due to fluctuations in the market. Indexed annuities do not carry such risk. Remember, EIAs are fixed annuities—the risk is borne by the insurer, not the contract holder. The contract holder's principal is secure.

Indexing also removes a typical impediment to the annuity sale, which is the "trust me" nature of renewal interest rates. As explained earlier, declared-rate annuities typically have interest rate guarantee periods of one year. At the same time, their surrender charge periods—the period following contract issue during which charges are assessed if the contract is cashed in—often last for 5 to 10 years. Therefore, the insurer is in a position to credit whatever interest rate it chooses (subject to policy minimums) during this period. Contract holders are in a position of limited liquidity and unable to easily or inexpensively withdraw or otherwise move their money if they are dissatisfied with the insurer's renewal interest rate. In effect then, the contract holder must "trust" that the insurer will be fair in crediting renewal rates.

Most EIAs remove the "trust me" element, in that the credited interest rate is not subject to the decision of the insurer, but is instead linked to equity market performance. The elimination of the "trust me" element is certainly one of the reasons that EIAs are popular. However, it is important to note that some EIAs do have an element of "trust me" in them: they contain participation rates and/or caps that are subject to adjustment by the carrier during the limited liquidity years. (These features are explained more fully in Chapters 3 and 4.)

■ DISTRIBUTION OF EQUITY INDEXED ANNUITIES

A full understanding of equity indexed annuities requires knowing how these products are sold. As is the case with all forms of annuities, there are a number of distribution channels that link the product and the consumer.

Distribution by Registered Reps

Equity indexed annuities were introduced to registered representatives of national stock brokerage firms (wirehouses), independent broker-dealer firms and regional brokerage firms in the early 1990s. Through wirehouses and regional firms, distribution of the product has not been widespread. By their very nature, these broker-dealer firms have, traditionally, focused on the sale of products that provide full access to market performance (albeit with the associate risk of principal); products with guaranteed principal and guaranteed interest rates had not been widely embraced. It took some time before stockbrokers in these types of firms learned how an EIA can be positioned in a client's retirement savings portfolio and understood its value as a "safe money" vehicle. Though sales of EIAs through these types of firms are increasing, it is at a moderate pace.

Sales of EIAs in the independent broker-dealer firms, however, is another matter. Independent broker-dealer firms employ or provide services to securities-licensed

> ### ILL. 1.3 ■ *EIA Sales by Registered Reps*
>
> Though it is popularly presumed that most life insurance agents do not hold a securities license, a random survey conducted in 1997 by NFC Consulting Group indicated that 79 percent of 174 agents who had sold an indexed annuity were registered representatives. The sales agents contacted represented a broad base of the brokerage general agency distribution channel rather than specific firms. In some regions of the country, the percentage of agents holding a securities license was as high as 80 percent; the lowest was 63 percent.

individuals who take a financial planning approach when working with clients as opposed to focusing on the sale of individual investment products. The EIA product was widely embraced in this channel from its introduction. Planners recognized early its value as an important part of a client's long-term financial or retirement plan. Independent broker-dealer firms continue to account for a large portion of EIA sales.

Distribution by Life Insurance Agents

At about the same time the EIA was introduced in the broker-dealer channel, it was also introduced to traditional life insurance agents. In this arena, there was immediate and widespread acceptance of the product. Life insurance agents are accustomed to marketing fixed annuities and life insurance products that provide safety of principal and interest rate guarantees. With EIAs, there is the added bonus of being able to offer the client a rate of return that is linked to the performance of the equity markets.

Since EIAs are not securities or stock market investments, an agent is not required to hold a securities license in order to sell these products. This too has accounted for some of the widespread popularity of EIAs within the life agent distribution channel. For the first time, agents who were not registered to sell securities could provide their clients with an opportunity to achieve potentially greater growth on their fixed annuities, without risk of market loss. Agents embraced this idea, and thus, became the largest distribution channel for EIAs.

Distribution by Banks

Equity indexed annuities were introduced to the bank distribution channel in the mid-1990s. Since that time, bank sales of EIAs have grown steadily. Many in the industry believe that banks will become a major distribution source for these products, because bank customers are typically risk averse and conservative. With their built-in guarantee of no market risk, EIAs are considered to be a perfect product for the bank annuity purchaser.

■ REGISTERED vs. NONREGISTERED STATUS OF EIAs

As noted, life insurance agents became the biggest sellers of EIAs in the mid- to late-1990s. EIA features are distinct, and the products fit a market niche not served by traditional fixed or variable annuities. In addition to this, the regulatory environment supports the fact that agents do not need to hold a securities license in order to sell most EIAs. It is important to understand why this is so.

Currently, the vast majority of EIAs on the market are fixed annuities not registered with the Securities and Exchange Commission (SEC). Those few that are registered differ from fixed EIAs in definition and structure. Registered annuities are sold with a prospectus, and the agent must hold either an NASD Series 6 or Series 7 license in order to sell them. Depending on the state, the agent may also have to pass the Series 63 examination, which covers the Uniform Securities Act.

The regulatory framework for determining whether an equity indexed annuity requires registration with the SEC as an investment product is found in Section 3(a)(8) of the Securities Act of 1933. Section 3(a)(8) provides a definition of an "insurance" product vis-á-vis a "securities" product. Further guidance is provided by the spirit of the SEC's 1986 "safe harbor" Rule 151. Rule 151 was created to assist courts and regulators in determining whether some of the newer types of hybrid insurance/investment contracts not in existence when Section 3(a)(8) was drafted constitute "insurance" within the meaning of Section 3(a)(8) or "securities" which would require registration under the 1933 act.

Rule 151 specifically states that an annuity is considered an insurance product that does not have to be registered as a security if it meets the following conditions:

1. It is issued by an insurance company.

2. The insurer assumes the investment risk.

   – The value of the contract won't vary with investment experience (as a variable annuity does).

   – A minimum rate of interest is credited to the contract (equal at least to the minimum nonforfeiture interest rate for individual annuities).

   – The current interest rate must be declared in advance and not modified more than once a year.

3. The contract cannot be marketed or sold primarily as an investment.

   – The contract must be marketed on the basis of stability and security.

   – Marketing must fairly and accurately describe both the insurance and investment features of a particular contract.

   – Marketing must emphasize the product's use as a long-term retirement or income security vehicle.

The equity indexed annuity represents a truly unique fixed annuity product. State insurance and federal securities regulators did not anticipate such a product when they set forth the rules and regulations regarding traditional fixed and variable annuity contracts. If they were to rely solely on a strict interpretation of Rule 151, no EIA would fully qualify as an insurance product, given the requirement that "the current interest rate must be declared in advance. . . ." As we will see in Chapter 4, this is not the case with EIAs. However, the spirit of this rule as well as some of the earlier court cases tried under Section 3(a)(8) provide insurance carriers with guidance regarding the nonregistered status of their products.

Ultimately, the decision to register or not register an EIA will depend upon its specific features. Generally, an EIA product is registered if it cannot guarantee safety from market risk. This is typical of products that contain a market value adjustment (MVA) feature that can invade principal and accumulated interest. In addition, there may be other reasons why some insurers have chosen to register their equity indexed annuities:

1. Their sales forces are securities-licensed and are accustomed to offering products sold by prospectus.

2. It offers more flexibility with regard to product design.

3. Marketing efforts can emphasize the product's investment aspects.

The contractual features of most EIAs on the market today place them outside the law's definition of a "security"; consequently, they do not have to be registered. It should be noted, however, that in 1997, the SEC sent out a "concept release" asking for information on how insurers were marketing EIAs. An SEC concept release is a request for information; it is not an indication of the SEC's position on a particular topic. The purpose of the concept release was to gather input to help the SEC clarify its thinking on the status of EIAs. The Commission is under no obligation to respond to the information submitted by the financial services industry. It might or it may never provide any formal guidance with regard to the regulatory status of EIAs. (At the time of this text's publication, the SEC had made no pronouncements in this matter.) Most insurers continue to rely on the opinions of their legal counsel and the current interpretations of Rule 151 and Section 3(a)(8) case law when determining the status of their equity indexed annuities.

■ SUMMARY

A truly unique product, the equity indexed annuity represents another option for those who seek a vehicle to house their long-term savings dollars. The EIA has all of the same features and safety attributes of a fixed annuity, most significantly the guarantee of principal. The primary distinction is that its interest rate is linked to a stock market index, typically the S&P 500. Consequently, an EIA contract holder has the opportunity to achieve potentially greater growth without risk to principal. Currently, the largest distribution channels for EIAs are life insurance agents and independent broker-dealers, but it is believed that banks will become a significant distribution channel in the near future.

■ **CHAPTER REVIEW QUESTIONS**

1. Which of the following correctly identifies the feature that most distinguishes an equity indexed annuity from a traditional fixed annuity?

    A. The short-term nature of the EIA contract

    B. The way in which interest is credited to the EIA contract

    C. The guarantee of principal associated with EIA products

    D. The minimum interest rate guarantee underlying the EIA contract

2. Most equity indexed products are sold through

    A. banks

    B. stockbrokers

    C. credit unions

    D. life insurance agents

3. An equity indexed annuity would most appropriately address which of the following needs?

    A. College funding

    B. Retirement

    C. Tax savings

    D. Short-term savings

4. Most equity indexed annuities on the market today are registered as securities.

    True or False

5. When marketing equity indexed annuities, the practitioner can rightfully liken an EIA to an investment in the stock market.

    True or False

2

Understanding Annuities

C hapter 1 served as an introduction to equity indexing and equity indexed annuities. To thoroughly understand these products, however, the practitioner must have a basic knowledge of annuities in general and how they serve the consumer in today's financial markets. Only by placing the EIA and the traditional annuity side by side can appropriate comparisons be made and differences fully understood. In this chapter, we will review the features and characteristics of traditional annuities and the reasons consumers purchase them.

■ ■ ■ ■ ■

■ THE PURPOSE OF ANNUITIES

In the simplest of terms, an annuity is a vehicle for accumulating funds and/or distributing a stream of income over a specified period of time. It is a cash contract with an insurance company, purchased through the payment of a single premium deposit or through a number of premium deposits, scheduled or unscheduled. The insurer invests the contract owner's premiums and credits the contract with a certain rate of return; the funds accumulate on a tax-deferred basis, which enhances their growth. The invested premiums plus the interest earned on the invested premiums create the annuity fund. At a certain point in the contract's term, the annuity is scheduled to "annuitize," at which point it will generate periodic payments from the annuity fund to the contract owner. These payments can be structured to extend over any specified period of time, including the owner's life. The individual whose life is used to measure the income stream and who is designated to receive the annuity payments is known as the annuitant.

The primary purpose annuities address is retirement savings and retirement planning. An annuity is a long-term planning product, suitable for those with long-term investment horizons. With few exceptions, they are inappropriate or inefficient for other needs or other objectives. However, the practitioner need not worry that this restricts the market—saving for retirement is one of the most pressing financial issues facing consumers today. The need for retirement planning and the application of annuities for this purpose are virtually unlimited.

■ TYPES OF ANNUITIES

There are many types of annuities and many variations and options available to annuity buyers. Basically, the defining characteristics of an annuity can be categorized by the following:

- how the annuity funds are invested;

- when the annuity payments begin; and

- method of premium payment.

How Annuity Funds Are Invested: Fixed vs. Variable

There are two options available to annuity buyers with regard to the investment of their funds: fixed or variable. The basic difference boils down to which party—the contract holder or the insurer—bears the risk with regard to the investment performance of these funds.

Fixed Annuities

A *fixed annuity* is designed to limit the contract holder's risk, including investment-related risk, by providing a guaranteed rate of return. Fixed annuities are backed by the insurer's general account assets, which are used to support its contractual guarantees and obligations. With insurance products that guarantee their values, the insurer assumes the investment risk, not the contract owner. In other words, the contract owner is guaranteed that his or her contract will provide the promised values and benefits, whether or not it earns the rate of return the insurer assumes it will. Consequently, to cover the benefits and guarantees these products provide, the insurer invests fixed contract funds in safe, secure investments. In turn, this allows a steady, albeit conservative, rate of return to be credited to the contract.

Variable Annuities

With a *variable annuity*, the insurance company gives the contract holder the option of having his or her premiums invested and managed differently. A variable annuity is typically supported by two investment accounts: a general (guaranteed) account, as described above, and a separate (variable) account. The general account provides a guaranteed return; the variable or separate account offers a variety of stock and bond subaccounts, which provide the potential for higher returns, but without any guarantees. The contract owner can determine how much of his or her premium is to be allocated to the general account and how much is to be allocated to the separate account.

A variable annuity gives the contract holder greater control over the investment of his or her premium monies, but it also means that the contract holder assumes the investment risk to the extent any premiums are invested in the separate account. In essence, because they determine account allocations, variable annuity owners can choose how much investment risk they are willing to take. Benefits from a variable annuity will ultimately be determined by the performance of the underlying separate account funds.

ILL. 2.1 ■ *Types of Annuities*

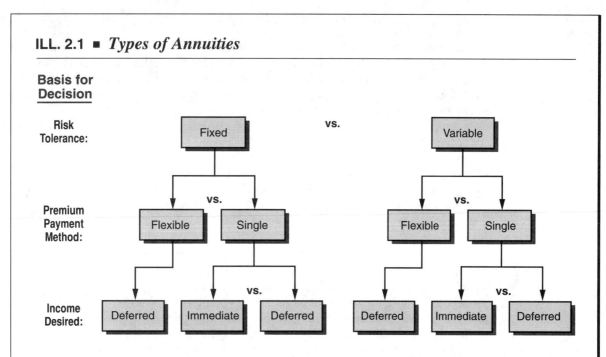

Basis for Decision

Risk Tolerance: Fixed vs. Variable

Premium Payment Method: Fixed → Flexible vs. Single; Variable → Flexible vs. Single

Income Desired: Flexible → Deferred; Single → Immediate vs. Deferred (for both Fixed and Variable)

There are many types of annuities, each designed to serve different purposes and fulfill different needs. A good way to chart these different annuities is to categorize them on the basis of the prospect's financial objectives. A *fixed annuity* provides for a guaranteed, fixed return and a fixed benefit; a *variable annuity* provides for a fluctuating return and benefit, in response to its underlying investments. Both fixed and variable annuities can be funded with *periodic premiums* or with a *single lump-sum premium.* If *immediate income* is desired, either annuity can be "annuitized" and converted to produce an income stream. If income is to be *deferred,* the annuity accumulates premiums and earnings, tax deferred, until a future point in time.

Because of the risk associated with variable annuity investments, they are considered "securities" and must be registered with the Securities and Exchange Commission. To sell variable annuities, practitioners must have a life insurance license as well as a Series 6 or 7 license. (In certain states, a Series 63 license is also required.)

The choice between investing in a fixed or variable annuity usually depends on the contract holder's risk tolerance. A fixed annuity places the investment risk on the insurer; a variable annuity means that the contract holder assumes the risk to the extent he or she invests in the contract's separate account. Each type of annuity has its advantages and drawbacks.

When Annuity Payments Begin: Immediate vs. Deferred

An annuity can be purchased for the sole purpose of distributing or liquidating a sum of money or it can be used as a vehicle to accumulate funds. This is the distinction between an immediate annuity and a deferred annuity.

Immediate Annuities

An *immediate annuity* is designed to generate an income stream to the annuitant almost immediately after it is purchased. As you might imagine, immediate annuity contracts can only be purchased or funded with a single lump-sum premium, which creates the annuity principal. Then, within a very short time, the contract annuitizes and begins to generate payments to the annuitant on a regular, structured basis. Each payment consists partly of principal and partly of interest earnings on the yet-to-be-distributed account balance.

The time period between an immediate annuity's purchase and the start of the payout is usually one month but never exceeds 13 months. Most annuity payments are made monthly; however, many insurers allow the annuitant to elect a quarterly, semiannual or annual payment schedule.

The duration of the annuity income flow and the amount of each payment depends on a number of factors. Obviously, the total amount of the annuity fund is one factor; another is the distribution, or settlement, option the contract holder selects. This option can be structured so that payments are made for a specified period of time such as 5, 10 or 20 years (a *term certain* option); they can be paid for the duration of the annuitant's life (a *life income* option); or they can be paid for the duration of two lives (a *joint and survivor* option). There are also variations of these payments that combine a term certain option with a life income option. Given a specified amount of annuity funds, the longer the period of income payments and the more guarantees the payout provides, the smaller the amount of each payment.

The income flow from immediate annuities can be either fixed or variable. Under a *fixed immediate annuity*, the annuitant is guaranteed a fixed income flow, with unchanging payments. For the annuitant, there is no risk of market fluctuations affecting the amount of income; the insurer absorbs the market risk associated with the investment of the annuity funds. A *variable immediate annuity* transfers the investment risk to the annuitant. This means that once an income stream begins, the payments will fluctuate, increasing or decreasing based on the performance of the underlying investments.

Regardless of the payout option, the primary purpose of an immediate annuity is to create an income stream. Its function is truly that of a *distribution*, or *liquidation*, vehicle.

Deferred Annuities

In contrast to the immediate annuity, the deferred annuity is characterized by an *accumulation period*. In other words, there is an extended period between the time the annuity contract is purchased and when it is scheduled to annuitize—typically, several years. The contract holder funds a deferred annuity by making periodic premium payments on a flexible schedule or through a single, lump-sum payment. If it is a typical *fixed deferred annuity*, the insurer guarantees the initial interest rate it will credit to the contract for a specified period, such as one year, three years or five years; beyond this initial period, renewal rates are subject to change. If it is a *variable deferred annuity*, the rate of return credited to the contract will depend on the performance of the separate account options in which the funds are invested.

Regardless of the investment configuration—fixed or variable—interest on deferred annuities is not taxable until it is withdrawn or distributed.

Most deferred annuities apply surrender charges for a specified number of years after the contract is purchased, in the event the contract holder cashes in or surrenders the contract before the insurer has recouped the cost of selling and issuing the contract.

At the point where the contract holder decides to access the deferred annuity cash value—usually at retirement—one of three distribution options can be elected:

1. a lump-sum distribution of the entire cash value;

2. annuitization, which converts the funds to an income stream (fixed or variable, like those described above); or

3. systematic withdrawals.

Each of these options is briefly described in Ill. 2.2.

Funding Method: Single Premium vs. Periodic Premiums

There are two ways in which an annuity can be funded: with a single, lump-sum payment or with a series of payments, made periodically over time.

Single-Premium Annuities

A single-premium annuity is purchased with a single lump-sum premium payment at the inception of the contract. In fact, most of the sales volume written in the annuity business today and in the past has been single premium in nature. A single-premium contract does not allow the contract holder to make additional deposits into the contract; the funding of the annuity is accomplished with one payment.

Periodic (Flexible) Premium Annuities

Annuities may also be funded with periodic premium payments, payable on a flexible schedule. For example, a flexible premium annuity might require a certain minimum initial premium—$500, for instance—but then allow the contract holder to make additional deposits of as little as $25 as often as he or she desires. Flexible premium annuities are used widely to fund individual retirement accounts (IRAs) and tax-sheltered annuities (TSAs).

■ FEATURES OF FIXED DEFERRED ANNUITIES

As the foregoing discussion indicates, annuities come in all different shapes and sizes. For purposes of understanding equity indexed annuities, however, the design that we need to focus on is the *fixed deferred annuity* since it represents the chassis upon which the EIA is built. Though slight differences exist, fixed deferred annuity

ILL. 2.2 ■ *Annuity Payout Options*

When the time comes to access the funds in their annuities, there are a number of options available to contract holders. These include lump-sum, annuitization and systematic withdrawals.

Lump-Sum Distribution

An owner of a deferred annuity has the right to cash in his or her contract and receive a lump-sum payment of the annuity funds. However, there are two important details annuity owners should be aware of. First, almost all deferred annuity contracts carry *surrender charges* during the first few years that are assessed if the owner surrenders the contract during the surrender charge period. The surrender charge applicable in any year is usually expressed as a percentage of the contract's accumulated value or the amount invested. Second, if a cash distribution is taken before the owner reaches age 59½, a 10 percent penalty may also be applied. This penalty is imposed to discourage the use of annuities as short-term tax-sheltered investments.

Annuitization

Annuitization converts the annuity funds into an income stream, payable in regular installments (usually monthly), for as long a period as the owner wishes. The income stream can be fixed, in which the amount of each payment is guaranteed and unchanging, or it can be variable, in which the amount of each payment varies according to the performance of the investments in which the funds are deposited. Annuitized income streams can be structured to extend for a definite period of years or for the life of the annuitant (or the joint lives of the annuitant and a beneficiary). Funds that are annuitized over a life expectancy are not subject to the 10 percent penalty, even if the income payments begin before the owner is age 59½.

Annuitized income payments are taxed according to a concept known as the *exclusion ratio*. Part of each payment the annuitant receives is considered to be a return of his or her principal, which is not taxed; the remaining portion of the payment consists of interest earnings, which is taxed. To this extent, annuitized payments are tax advantaged, since a portion of each is excluded from taxation.

Systematic Withdrawals

An alternative to annuitization, systematic withdrawals provide a way for an annuity owner to receive income payments without being locked into a fixed payment schedule. The funds are available to the owner, from which he or she can take withdrawals at any time and in any amount. This option provides far more flexibility than annuitization, which irrevocably commits the annuity fund to liquidation. However, the tax treatment of systematic withdrawals is different than that of annuitization. There is no tax-advantaged exclusion ratio; all withdrawals are fully taxable until the fund's earnings are depleted. After that, of course, withdrawal of principal is not taxable.

products as a whole are characterized by certain features that are consistent from product to product. It is important to understand these features in order to understand EIAs.

Maturity Date

Every fixed annuity contract specifies a *maturity date*. The maturity, or annuity, date is the date on which annuitized payments are scheduled to begin. In most contracts, the maturity date is the later of 10 contract years or the contract anniversary that falls in the year the annuitant reaches age 85. It should be noted that most insurers will allow the deferral period to continue for some time past the maturity date, if the contract holder requests.

Death Benefit

Most deferred annuity contracts provide for the payment of a *death benefit* in the event the contract holder or the annuitant dies before the contract's maturity date. The benefit is typically expressed as the amount of premiums paid, less any withdrawals, or the contract's accumulated value, if greater.

Surrender Charges

Almost all fixed deferred annuities have *surrender charges*. These charges are assessed during the early years of the contract should the contract holder liquidate or surrender the annuity before the insurer has had an opportunity to recover the cost of issuing the contract. In the past, it was common to find surrender charges applied for the duration of the contract; today, most deferred annuities assess surrender charges for only a limited period of time after contract issue. The average duration of a contract's surrender charge period is about 8 years, with most surrender charges falling within a range of 5 to 10 years.

There are a number of ways in which insurers assess surrender charges. The most common are described in Ill. 2.3.

Interest Rates

As explained in the previous chapter, fixed deferred annuities are credited with a specified rate of interest, which is usually based on prevailing market rates. The most common approach is to establish the interest rate on a policy anniversary date and guarantee that rate until the next policy anniversary date which, for most contracts, is a year later. At that point a renewal rate is declared, which is fixed and guaranteed for that next year. For example, assume that Louise deposited $35,000 in a fixed deferred annuity and, at issue, the declared interest rate payable on her contract was 8.5 percent. This means that the interest credited to Louise's contract that first year would be $2,975. For the second contract year, the insurer declares a renewal rate of 7.75 percent; interest credited to Louise's contract that second year would amount to $2,943.* The renewal rate process for the third and subsequent years would be similar. The interest rate that is declared for any one year is guaranteed for that year.

Underlying every fixed annuity contract is a guaranteed *minimum* interest rate. This minimum reflects, in part, the reserving and nonforfeiture requirements every insurer must meet and effectively represents a "worst case" scenario relative to the return an annuity contract will earn. For most fixed annuities, the minimum rate is

---

* This is a very simplified example. The initial premium deposit of $35,000 is credited with 8.5 percent interest, which produces $2,975 in earnings. This amount, added to the $35,000 principal, is then credited with a 7.75 percent rate of return, producing $2,943 in earnings for the second year: $35,000 × .085 = $2,975; ($2,975 + $35,000) × .0775 = $2,943.

ILL. 2.3 ■ *Deferred Annuity Surrender Charges*

Surrender charges are common to most deferred annuity products and are usually expressed in one of three ways: as a percentage of account value, as a percentage of premium deposit or as a loss of interest. The chart illustrates how each of these methods operates. Each assumes an initial premium deposit of $100,000 and an 8 percent return credited to the contract.

		Premium Deposit Method	*Account Value Method*	*Loss of Interest Method*
Surrender Charges by Year		7%, 6%, 5%, 4%, 3%, 2%, 1%, 0%	4%, 4%, 4%, 4%, 4%, 4%, 0%	Six months' loss of interest
Basis of Surrender Charge		Percentage of premium	Percentage of accumulated account value	Annual interest
Amount of Surrender Charge	Year 1	$7,000	$4,320	$4,000
	Year 2	$6,000	$4,666	$4,320
	Year 3	$5,000	$5,039	$4,666
	Year 4	$4,000	$5,442	$5,039
	Year 5	$3,000	$5,877	$5,442
	Year 6	$2,000	$6,348	$5,878
	Year 7	$1,000	$ 0	$ 0
	Year 8+	$ 0		

3 percent to 4 percent. An annuity's declared interest rate will never be less than the minimum.

How Annuity Interest Rates Are Determined

There are many ways in which insurers invest annuity funds and credit interest to their fixed contracts. While a complete discussion of interest-crediting is beyond the scope of this text, it is important to understand a few basic principles.

From an investment standpoint, an annuity is an asset-management product. Contract holders place their annuity premiums with an insurance company, where they are pooled with funds from other contract holders. The insurer invests those premiums—typically in fixed rate instruments such as bonds and mortgages—and earns a certain rate of return. Out of this return, the insurer must cover the costs of issuing the contracts (including commissions) and generate a profit. The remainder is available to credit to its annuity contracts. The difference between what the insurer earns on its investments and what interest rate it credits to its annuities is known as the "spread."

In a stable interest rate environment, renewal rates on traditional fixed annuities should not vary significantly from year to year. However, as noted in Chapter 1, the traditional fixed annuity has often been called the "trust me" annuity because the

---

ILL. 2.4 ■ *Declared Rate Annuity Interest Crediting*

A fixed annuity is an asset-management product. The rate the insurer earns on its investments drives the rate of interest that it credits to its annuity contracts.

9.00%	Rate of interest insurer is able to earn on its investments
–1.75%	Cost of issuing contract and generating a profit
7.25%	Rate of interest credited by insurer to its annuities

---

contract owner has to trust that the insurer will credit fair and competitive rates at each renewal. Due to surrender charges, which can extend years into the contract, the contract holder has little recourse if reasonable renewal rates are not declared. This is one drawback to traditional fixed annuities that equity indexed annuities can overcome.

Liquidity Options Prior to Maturity

Most fixed deferred annuities today offer a number of ways that contract holders can access their annuity funds prior to contract maturity. These include *free withdrawals*, *policy loans* and withdrawals taken due to *illness* or *hospitalization*.

Free Withdrawals

The *free withdrawal* provision was introduced in the late 1970s and is now common in most fixed annuity contracts. It allows the contract holder to withdraw up to a stipulated amount—most commonly 10 percent of the contract's accumulated value—every year without incurring surrender charges. The duration of the free withdrawal provision extends for the same number of years that surrender charges apply.

Free withdrawal privileges are typically not cumulative. In other words, if the privilege is not exercised in any given contract year, the unused benefit may not be added to the next contract year's benefit.

Policy Loans

A second form of liquidity, though not widely available, is through *policy loans*. In a typical policy loan arrangement, the insurer allows the contract holder to borrow up to 75 percent of his or her accumulated contract values. A minimum interest rate is typically assessed. For example, the insurer might charge the difference between the credited rate on the contract and the current rate on Moody's AAA Corporate Bond Index, with a minimum charge of 1 percent. (Policy loans are most common in 403(b) annuity plans marketed to teachers and administrators.)

Nursing Home, Hospitalization and Terminal Illness Provisions

Relatively new to annuity contracts are provisions that allow contract holders to withdraw all or some of their contract values free of surrender charges if the contract holder is confined to a nursing home or hospital or diagnosed as terminally ill. These provisions are still being developed and refined and each carrier treats this form of liquidity differently.

Early Withdrawals and Taxes

Although deferred annuity contract holders can easily access their contract values, there could be significant tax consequences for doing so. Any annuity withdrawal or distribution attributed to interest earnings that is taken before age 59½ is subject to a 10 percent penalty. This penalty is not applied if the distribution is taken as a life annuity, as will be discussed later in this chapter.

■ WHY PEOPLE BUY ANNUITIES

Having reviewed traditional annuity features, we are now ready to explore the various reasons people buy annuities. As is the case with any financial product, annuities offer a number of benefits that appeal to a wide variety of consumers. However, for most, the reasons to purchase a fixed annuity boil down to four: safety (in terms of the product itself as well as the industry that delivers it), tax deferral, liquidity and probate efficiency. Let's look at each.

Safety: An Insurance Industry Standard

The principal reason individuals choose a fixed annuity as an investment is *safety*. The insurance industry has long been recognized as safe, sound and secure, more than capable of backing the promises and guarantees associated with its fixed products. Insurers have gone to great lengths to protect their contract holders and their fixed investments. As a result, only once in the industry's history have owners of fixed annuities lost money.*

Why is the fixed annuity such a safe investment? How are insurers able to make the guarantees they do? The answer lies in the industry's *legal reserve system*.

Legal Reserve System

The legal reserve system was developed specifically to protect annuity contract holders (as well as insurance policy owners) through prudent asset management and accounting practices. It has been in existence in this country since the beginning of the 20th century.

At the heart of the legal reserve system are the statutory reserves that every insurance company must establish to protect its contracts and contract holders. It is what

---

*This occurred in 1991 when Executive Life failed.

the insurer must have available to meet its obligations and claims, based on the contractual provisions of its annuities and life insurance contracts. Insurance company reserving and accounting are extremely complicated, technical subjects; however, a basic knowledge of the system can be helpful when making relative comparisons of the annuity to other investments that your clients or prospects may be considering. Important points that should be noted are the difference between *capital*, *surplus* and *reserves* and how they relate to the safety of the annuity investment.

Capital and Surplus.   Capital and surplus are, in essence, the net worth of an insurance company. Generally speaking, they are the assets of the insurer minus its liabilities. To maintain the integrity of the reserve system, companies may periodically increase reserves in recognition of losses or potential losses in their investment portfolios. Also, the company uses capital and surplus to invest in the writing of new business and relies on them as a safety buffer for emergencies. As a whole, the capital and surplus of the insurance industry, as a percentage of assets, is currently about 8 percent.

Reserves.   Reserves are liabilities of an insurance company, representing funds set aside to meet the company's contractual obligations. They are invested by the insurer and backed by its assets. Reserves are subject to creditors but only after all contract holder claims have been resolved. Obviously, this provides great safety to the contract holder, whose claim is placed ahead of bondholders and shareholders.

When overseen by state regulators, the balance between surplus and reserves provides a remarkable degree of safety, unparalleled in the investment world. Under the watchful eye and careful monitoring by the National Association of Insurance Commissioners, the insurance industry remains one of an elite group of industries not under the federal government's control. This is, in large part, the result of the efficient solvency system currently in place.

State Guaranty Funds

Each of the 50 states has enacted legislation to protect the contract holders of that state should an insurance company be faced with insolvency. This legislation resulted in the creation of 50 *guaranty funds*, required by the state but funded by the insurance companies that are admitted to do business in that state. Most state guaranty funds assess their admitted insurers an additional charge to cover any carrier insolvencies within the state. Different states have different limits of protection.

It is important to emphasize that these state guaranty funds provide the contract holder with protection without federal or state funding. All guaranty associations are funded by insurance companies and administered by the states. However, practitioners should check with their states to confirm limitations and to determine whether or not they even have the right to disclose the existence of the guaranty fund. Many states do not allow disclosure of guaranty fund information to potential contract holders because they do not want insurers and producers to rely on the fund and its guarantees when designing and marketing products. To do so could lead to abuse of the guaranty associations.

Guarantee of Principal

Safety of principal in any investment is affected by a number of risks. Interest rates, business cycles, price levels, consumer confidence—any or all of these things can affect the value of an investment. *Market risk* (sometimes called *asset value fluctuation*) is the adjustment that occurs in the value of an asset as outside influences, such as interest rates and business risk, affect the underlying market value of that investment. However, regardless of these risks, fixed annuity contracts guarantee to return 100 percent of the contract holder's principal, less any withdrawals or loans. This contractual guarantee does not eliminate the risk or the asset value fluctuation per se, but assures that the contract holder's risk is limited only to the interest earned within the contract. This is a significant advantage the annuity has over alternative investments such as corporate or municipal bonds.

A bond is an "IOU." A bond investor lends money to a corporation or municipality and in exchange receives the bond which states that a certain rate of interest will be paid for the use of the investor's money until a specified maturity date, at which time the principal is returned to the investor. For example, let's say XY&Z Corporation issued a $1,000 bond last year that pays a fixed rate of 7 percent annually and matures in 15 years. An individual who purchased this bond would receive interest payments of $70 a year. At the bond's maturity in 15 years, the bondholder would return the bond to XY&Z and would receive $1,000 in cash.

Bonds may be held to maturity or they may be sold prior to maturity. However, the price of a bond may fluctuate between issuance and maturity; a $1,000 bond may not always sell for $1,000. This is due to the inverse relationship that exists between bond prices and market interest rates. The interest rate designated on the bond certificate is fixed, payable for the duration of the bond term, but the market value of the bond is determined by the interest rate at the time of sale. For example, whereas the 7 percent payable on the XY&Z bond was likely competitive with interest rates offered by other bond-issuing companies at that time, if overall interest rates have changed since XY&Z issued that bond, the market value (price) of the bond will reflect this inversely. If interest rates have gone up, the market value of the bond will decrease (the bond will sell at a "discount"); if interest rates have gone down, the market value price of the bond will increase (the bond will sell at a "premium"). This is the risk bondholders must absorb that annuity owners do not.

Let's look at an example. Assume that three years ago, Kathy made three investments: a $100,000 short-term bond paying 7 percent interest, a $100,000 intermediate-term bond paying 7.6 percent interest and a $100,000 fixed deferred annuity crediting 8 percent interest. If interest rates remain stable, there is no asset value fluctuation and all three investments perform to meet Kathy's needs. But what if interest rates increase slowly by 1 percent a year for the next three years? Now, new short-term and intermediate-term bonds are yielding 10 percent and 10.6 percent, respectively, and new annuity contracts are crediting 11 percent. Kathy, who is still earning 8 percent on her annuity and is locked into her bond rates, is no longer happy and wishes to exchange all three of her investments to get the higher interest rates.

The problem is that Kathy must get someone else to buy her bonds, which are paying 7 percent and 7.6 percent while new issues within the bond market are 3 percent higher. Obviously, there is a price to pay for this liquidity; her bonds must be sold

ILL. 2.5 ■ *When Interest Rates Rise, Bond Values Decline*

	Cost	Initial Rate	Value* (After 3% increase in interest rates)
Short-term bond	$100,000	7.0%	$94,681
Intermediate-term bond	$100,000	7.6%	$83,442

* This value is the equivalent of the present value of the remaining interest plus the $100,000 principal. The short-term bond has a 5-year maturity; the intermediate-bond has a 12-year maturity.

at a discount. As Ill. 2.5 shows, Kathy will lose $5,319 when she sells her short-term bond and more than $16,500 when she sells her intermediate-term bond.

This will not be the case with the annuity (unless the annuity has a market value adjustment feature). A fixed annuity contract provides that the insurer absorbs the market risk and, no matter what the fluctuating value of the market may indicate, the contract holder will always get back his or her principal. Consequently, Kathy would be able to transfer the annuity values—now, $125,971, less any surrender charges—to another carrier, if she wants to preserve tax deferral and receive a higher rate of return on her investment. In any event, if her principal is guaranteed, her full $100,000 would be returned, regardless of surrender charges.

Tax Deferral

> *From the standpoint of the contract holder, a deferred annuity, during its accumulation period, does not significantly differ from a long-term certificate of deposit (which, incidentally, also may be subject to penalty if it is surrendered prematurely) or any other portfolio investment which may be reduced to cash at any time. Nevertheless, interest from other portfolio investments is taxed currently whereas earnings credited to a deferred annuity are not. To the extent that annuities can be fashioned to offer interest rates that are competitive with rates paid by other financial instruments, there is little reason why a potential investor should purchase anything but a deferred annuity.*
>
> *Hon. John E. Chopoton, Assistant Secretary for Tax Policy, testifying before the Senate Finance Committee, March 30, 1980*

This quote goes straight to the heart of the second benefit annuities offer: the accumulation of funds on a *tax-deferred basis*, which maximizes the return. Tax deferral added to interest earnings can produce sizeable sums over time. For example, assume Gene, age 45, has $100,000 and is considering three investments: a one-year CD, a money-market fund and a deferred annuity. As shown below, the before-tax yields on these investments are 6.5 percent, 6.1 percent and 7.75 percent, respectively. (The higher rate on the annuity is reflective of the long-term nature of the contract.) However, Gene must pay current income taxes on the interest earnings of the CD and money-market fund. Consequently, because Gene is a 40 percent taxpayer (combined state and federal), the net yields on these investments drop to 3.9 percent and 3.66 percent, respectively. But the yield on the annuity, because of tax deferral, remains at 7.75 percent. This gives the annuity a significant advantage over the other two investments:*

	Certificate of Deposit	*Money-Market Fund*	*Annuity*
Before-tax yield:	6.5%	6.1%	7.75%
After-tax yield:	3.9%	3.66%	7.75%
1 year	$103,900	$103,660	$107,750
5 years	$121,081	$119,689	$145,240
10 years	$146,607	$143,255	$210,947
15 years	$177,514	$171,461	$306,379
20 years	$214,937	$205,221	$444,985

The difference between these investment options becomes very apparent when the 10-year and 20-year figures are examined. Over time, tax deferral puts the annuity far ahead of the alternatives. Even assuming a "worse case" scenario, wherein Gene liquidates his annuity after 20 years and takes his values in a lump sum (as opposed to annuitizing) and must pay taxes all at once on his earnings, the tax would amount to $137,994, leaving Gene with almost $307,000. By comparison, the CD—the nearest alternative—is almost $92,000 less in value.

Practitioners who are effective in selling the concept of an annuity's tax deferral have learned to calculate and explain *taxable equivalent yields*. A taxable equivalent yield is what a taxable investment must yield to make that investment equal to a tax-deferred investment. If the current yield on an annuity is 8 percent, for example, an individual who is in the 31 percent tax bracket would have to earn 11.59 percent on a comparable taxable investment to produce an equivalent yield after tax. The formula for determining the taxable equivalent yield is fairly simple:

$$\frac{\text{Tax-deferred yield}}{100\% - \text{Investor tax bracket}} = \text{Taxable equivalent yield}$$

The tax-deferred status annuities enjoy is one of their primary benefits. The trade-off is the long-term nature of the product and the holding period required. Annuity funds that are withdrawn before the owner reaches age 59½ are subject to penalty as well as tax, as explained in Ill. 2.6.

---

* All three investments assume the same rate of return over 20 years and annual compounding. After 20 years, the annuity value after taxes is $306,991.

ILL. 2.6 ■ *Taxation of Annuities*

How annuities are taxed is an important consideration. Following is an overview of the key issues.

Taxation During Accumulation

One of the benefits annuities offer is the tax-deferred accumulation of funds: while funds remain in the contract, no income tax is imposed on the interest earnings credited to the contract nor on the values as they build within the contract. This greatly enhances the accumulation of funds. However, in exchange for this favorable tax treatment, the annuity is considered a long-term retirement savings vehicle. If contract values are withdrawn before the owner is age 59½, a 10 percent penalty may be imposed on interest earnings taken, in addition to ordinary income tax. Let's say, for example, that at the age of 40, Alan deposited $25,000 in a fixed annuity. Now, eight years later, he withdraws $10,000. What is Alan's tax liability? To the extent the $10,000 represents interest earnings, he would have to pay a penalty of 10 percent on the withdrawal in addition to ordinary income taxes.

Annuity withdrawals prior to a contract's maturity are treated on a LIFO ("last-in, first-out") basis. In other words, withdrawals are considered to consist of interest earnings first. Only after all interest has been recovered is invested principal considered to be withdrawn. Using the example above, let's assume that the value of Alan's annuity at the time he took the $10,000 withdrawal was $40,000: $25,000 principal and $15,000 accumulated interest earnings. Consequently, the full amount of the $10,000 withdrawal would be deemed interest earnings, fully subject to the 10 percent penalty and ordinary income tax. This same tax treatment would apply to any amount Alan might withdraw up to $15,000; above $15,000, withdrawals would be considered a nontaxable return of principal.

The above example is based on the assumption that Alan's annuity is nonqualified. If it were a traditional IRA, the $25,000 in principal too would be subject to the 10 percent penalty and ordinary income tax, to the extent that any of it had been previously deducted as IRA contributions. There are, however, a number of exceptions to the 10 percent penalty for IRA withdrawals. These include withdrawals due to death, disability, qualifying medical expenses, first-time home purchase, payment of health insurance premiums while unemployed or when the withdrawal is taken as substantially equal payments over life.

Taxation of Annuitized Income

Income received from a (nonqualified) annuity under a structured annuitization option—single life, joint and survivor, term certain—is taxed according to the *exclusion ratio*. The exclusion ratio treats each annuity payment as part principal and part interest and applies a formula that defines and excludes the principal portion of the payment, taxing only the interest. This formula is equal to the "investment in the contract" (i.e., total premiums paid) divided by the "expected return" (i.e., total amount of annuitized income the owner is expected to receive under the income option he or she selected). For example, let's say that Bernice invested a total of $18,000 in a fixed deferred annuity. Now, at the age of 62, she opts to annuitize her contract and selects a single life payout, which will generate $150 a month for her life. Based on her life expectancy (22.5 years), the total expected payout under the contract is $40,500. The nontaxable portion of her annuity income is calculated as follows:

$$\frac{\$18,000 \text{ (investment in the contract)}}{\$40,500 \text{ (expected return)}} = 44.4 \text{ percent}$$

Consequently, $66.60 of each $150 annuity payment is excluded from income tax; the balance is taxable. This methodology applies until the entire investment in the contract has been paid out. If Bernice lives beyond her life expectancy, the annuity payments will continue; however, at that point they will consist entirely of interest and will be fully taxable. (For contracts that annuitized prior to 1987, the exclusion ratio continues indefinitely, permanently excluding from tax a portion of all annuity payments.)

The exclusion ratio applies to fixed annuity payouts. Annuitization of EIA contracts is exactly the same as annuitization of declared-rate annuity contracts. Consequently, for tax purposes, annuitized payments under an EIA will be treated in the same way.

Liquidity

Another benefit offered by fixed annuities is *liquidity*. As discussed earlier, there are a number of ways in which deferred annuity owners can access the values in their contracts prior to maturity: through free withdrawals, loans or a waiver of surrender charges if the owner is confined to a nursing home or hospital. The most extreme form of liquidity is a full surrender. As long as the contract does not specifically preclude surrender—and most do not—the owner can always terminate the policy for its surrender value, which is typically expressed as the amount equal to premium deposits plus interest minus free withdrawals minus surrender charges. The surrender value is almost always guaranteed not to invade principal.

Probate Efficiency

The final reason why annuities are so popular is that they bypass probate. *Probate* is the process that a state uses to identify assets within a decedent's estate for purposes of determining tax liability, executing the will and distributing property to beneficiaries and heirs. It provides for the payment of claims to a decedent's creditors and for disposal of the estate's assets. The process of probating an estate often entails publicity, delay and expense—none of which an annuity is subject to. Because an annuity is a contract, it bypasses the probate process. Annuity proceeds pass directly and immediately to the named beneficiary by virtue of the provisions of the contract and not through the process of probate.

■ SUMMARY

In this chapter, we reviewed the features and characteristics of the traditional fixed annuity and examined the many benefits it offers. The purpose was to establish a foundation for an understanding of the equity indexed annuity because an EIA *is* a fixed annuity. The EIA offers all of the benefits of its traditional counterpart— safety, guarantee of principal, tax deferral, liquidity and probate efficiency—with the added advantage of interest linked to equity market returns. This distinguishing feature of the EIA will be explored in Chapter 3.

■ CHAPTER REVIEW QUESTIONS

1. A fixed annuity is characterized by a provision that allows the contract holder to choose from a variety of mutual fund options for the investment of his or her premiums.

    True or False

2. An annuity will generally have a lower interest rate than a one-year certificate of deposit.

    True or False

3. All of the following are benefits associated with the traditional fixed annuity EXCEPT

    A. guarantee of principal

    B. investment returns based on the general direction of equity markets

    C. tax deferral on investment earnings

    D. probate efficiency

4. Louise, a 31 percent taxpayer, is considering a tax-deferred annuity investment that would yield an 8 percent rate of return. For her, what is the equivalent taxable yield on a taxable investment?

    A. 5.52 percent

    B. 5.60 percent

    C. 10.48 percent

    D. 11.59 percent

5. With regard to the rate of return a contract holder earns on his or her traditional fixed annuity, which of the following statements is true?

    A. The contract holder is credited with the lesser of the contract's minimum rate or the current declared rate.

    B. The contract holder is credited with the greater of the contract's minimum rate or the current declared rate.

    C. The contract's minimum rate is guaranteed only for the period during which surrender charges apply.

    D. The contract's current declared rate is guaranteed only for the period during which surrender charges apply.

6. A standard free withdrawal provision for traditional fixed annuities specifies

    A. free withdrawals are allowed after 10 years

    B. free withdrawals equal to 10 percent of the contract's value are allowed each year

    C. 10 percent of any withdrawal is subject to surrender charges

    D. 10 percent of any withdrawal is free of surrender charges

7. A typical minimum rate for a fixed annuity is 2 percent.

    True or False

3

Features of Equity Indexed Annuities

T hough EIA products are fixed annuities, there are a number of ways in which they differ from their declared-rate counterparts. In this chapter, we will focus on what sets equity indexed annuities apart and what characterizes these unique products. Not every EIA on the market today will have all of the characteristics we will be discussing; however, an understanding of the basic features is in order.

■ ■ ■ ■ ■

■ INDEXED INTEREST RATES

The most significant feature that differentiates equity indexed annuities from their traditional counterparts is that the interest credited to these contracts is based on a market index. For most EIAs, that index is the Standard & Poor's 500. There are a number of reasons why this is the index of choice. First of all, the S&P 500 is a widely recognized and widely available index. By measuring the price changes of 500 stocks which represent approximately 70 percent of the entire equity market in this country, it is a broad indicator of the overall stock market performance in the United States. These stocks are traded on the New York Stock Exchange (NYSE), the American Stock Exchange (AMEX) and the National Association of Securities Dealers Automated Quotation system (Nasdaq).

The S&P 500 identifies different economic "sectors" that are important to our nation's equity markets (including, for example, basic materials, capital goods, communication services, energy, technology and transportation). These sectors are divided into various industry groups, which are represented by leading companies. It is the stock of these leading companies that make up the index. The S&P 500 is considered so significant a benchmark for stock market performance that in 1968, the index became a component of the U.S. Department of Commerce's Index of Leading Economic Indicators, which is used to signal potential important turning points in the U.S. economy.

The S&P 500 is utilized by many financial services organizations today. Banks, mutual fund companies and insurance carriers all offer a wide range of financial instruments and products linked to the index. These products encompass both public and private (institutional) mutual funds, unit investment trusts, indexed-linked CDs and, of course, equity-linked life insurance and annuity products. More than $600 billion in public and institutional funds is linked to the S&P 500.

The S&P 500 is what is known as a "market-value weighted" index. This simply means that the value of the index is determined by multiplying, for each company included in the index, the number of shares outstanding by the individual stock prices. Because the S&P 500 is a market-value weighted index, each company's influence on its performance is directly proportional to its market value.

Calculating the yield that changes in the index's value generate is accomplished with a simple formula:

$$\frac{EP - BP}{BP}$$

where EP is the value of the index at the end of the period being measured and BP is the value of the index at the beginning of the period being measured.

For example, if the value of the S&P 500 is 1000 on January 1 and on December 31, the value is 1200, the yield for that year is 20 percent:

$$\frac{1200 - 1000}{1000} = .20$$

Had the S&P dropped by 100 points, the yield for that year would be a negative 10 percent:

$$\frac{900 - 1000}{1000} = -.10$$

Investment products with their rates of return tied to the S&P 500 would thus reflect, in some measure, this performance.

Clients purchasing financial products that are linked to the S&P 500 can check the performance of the index in the *Wall Street Journal, USA Today* and many regional and local newspapers. The value of the S&P 500 is also reported daily during the business segment of most television and radio news programs. Another important reason insurers utilize the S&P 500 for their indexed annuities is that there is a large and liquid options market for the index. The size and liquidity of the options market is of extreme importance to the insurer, as it is through the use of options that insurers are able to provide an indexed interest rate on their EIA products. (We will cover this topic in Chapter 5.)

Other Indexes

There are a few indexed annuities that do not utilize the S&P 500; instead, they use a potpourri of small cap and international indexes. With regard to the latter, most countries have indexes for their own stock markets, much like the S&P 500. A few insurance carriers have pieced together customized composite indexes composed of

ILL. 3.1 ■ *S&P 500 Reporting*

Following is an example of how the S&P 500 is reported daily. Taken from the *Wall Street Journal,* it reflects index values as of September 21, 1998.

High	Low	Close	Net Change	From Dec.31	% Change
1022.01	1011.86	1020.09	+1.22	+49.66	+5.1
This column indicates the highest average price the 500 stocks reached during the day.	This column indicates the lowest average price the 500 stocks reached during the day.	This column indicates the value of the index at the close of the day.	This column indicates the actual numeric change in the value of the index for that day.	This column indicates the actual numeric change in the value of the index from Dec. 31 of the previous year.	This column indicates the change in the value of the index from Dec. 31 of the previous year to the current day.

these international indexes. For instance, a composite international index might consist of indexes from Japan, the United Kingdom, Germany and France, each of which is given an equal weight. Theoretically, this approach represents a balanced, diversified international custom index and allows the EIA buyer to participate in the returns of overseas securities.

Dow Jones Indexes

It should come as no surprise that Dow Jones Indexes are being considered as potential alternatives for equity indexed products. The Dow Jones Industrial Average (DJIA), the Dow Jones Transportation Average (DJTA) and the Dow Jones Utility Average (DJUA) have long been considered leading indicators of the stock market's movement, offering various means by which the general course of the stock market can be measured and benchmarks against which individual stocks can be compared. The DJIA, the oldest and probably the most well-known index, represents 30 large capitalization blue-chip stocks, which account for approximately one-fifth of the market value of all U.S. stocks. The companies whose stocks are included in the DJIA are all leaders in their industries and their stocks are widely held and traded. This provides a measure of timeliness to the average since, at any point during the market's trading day, the DJIA reflects very recent transactions. (Stocks that were in the DJIA at the end of 1998 are listed in Ill. 3.3.)

The options market for the Dow Indexes is expanding rapidly, and insurance carriers may soon have another large and liquid source with which to hedge their EIA products.

Contrasted with the S&P 500 Index, the DJIA is price weighted as opposed to market-value weighted. In other words, within the index high-priced stocks carry more weight than lower-priced stocks. A 3 percent change in the price of stock at $100 a share will have a greater impact on the DJIA than a 3 percent change in the

---

ILL. 3.2 ■ *About the S&P 500 Index*

The history of the S&P 500 goes back to 1923 when Standard & Poor's introduced a series of indexes that included 233 companies and covered 26 industries. The modern S&P 500 was introduced on March 1, 1957, and contained 425 industrial stocks, 60 utilities and 15 railroads. Today, the index includes 383 industrials, 11 transportation stocks, 69 financials and 37 utility issues. Since 1988, the number of companies in each major industry sector has varied so that the S&P Index Committee can react appropriately to an increasingly dynamic economy and stock market.

How Stocks Within the Index Are Chosen

Standard & Poor's has an S&P Index Committee that is responsible for making changes in the index. Though Standard & Poor's as a company has many other business operations and interests, the management of the S&P 500 Index remains independent of those other interests. The S&P Index Committee reviews candidates on an on-going basis. Companies are not removed or added to the index based upon performance. Instead, they might be removed due to a merger, acquisition or possibly a bankruptcy filing. They might be added based on market value, industry group classification, market capitalization and how much trading activity the company's stock experiences. The S&P Index Committee strives to minimize the turnover and composition of the S&P 500 Index as much as possible.

Representative S&P 500 Companies

Following is a list of 20 companies in the S&P 500 Index. According to Standard & Poor's, these companies were among those with the highest market capitalizations (as of September 1998.)

• American International Group	• Intel Corporation
• AT&T Corporation	• Johnson & Johnson
• Bell Atlantic	• Lilly (Eli) & Company
• Bristol-Myers Squibb	• Merck & Company
• Coca-Cola Company	• Microsoft Corporation
• DuPont	• Pfizer Inc.
• Exxon Corporation	• Philip Morris
• General Electric	• Procter & Gamble
• Hewlett Packard	• Royal Dutch Petroleum
• IBM	• Wal-Mart Stores

---

price of stock at $20 a share. This means that if a particular stock moves up or down, it will have the same effect on the DJIA that it has on the stock itself. By contrast, in the S&P 500, a change in the price of a stock is multiplied by the number of outstanding shares of that stock. Thus, a 3 percent change in the price of a stock with a small market value will have a much smaller impact than a 3 percent change in the price of a stock with a large market value.

ILL. 3.3 ■ *Dow Jones Industrial Average Stocks*

- AT&T Corporation
- Allied Signal
- Aluminum Co. of America
- American Express
- Boeing
- Caterpillar
- Chevron
- Citigroup
- Coca-Cola
- Walt Disney
- DuPont
- Eastman Kodak
- Exxon Corporation
- General Electric
- General Motors

- Goodyear Tire & Rubber
- Hewlett Packard
- IBM
- International Paper
- Johnson & Johnson
- McDonalds
- Merck & Company
- 3M
- J.P. Morgan & Company
- Philip Morris
- Procter & Gamble
- Sears, Roebuck & Company
- Union Carbide
- United Technologies
- Wal-Mart Stores

A Word of Caution

It is expected that the use of other indexes for EIAs will continue to increase. However, some caution is necessary. First, these products should be kept simple and straightforward. If they become too complicated or if they employ indexes with which the targeted buyer is not familiar, sales will likely decrease. Second, the vast majority of equity indexed annuities today are fixed, nonregistered products with limited investment aspects. EIA designers must remember that the market for these products is typically a conservative, fixed annuity buyer looking for safety and some additional upside potential. Simplicity and understandability are paramount.

The Issue of Dividends

It is important to know that virtually all listed indexes, including the S&P 500, are *price* indexes, reflecting only increases and decreases in the price of the stocks in the index. They do not include dividends on the stocks or the reinvestment of dividends. Consequently, EIAs that tie their return to the S&P 500 will not reflect the effects of dividends. This is important since dividends can have a dramatic effect on total return over a number of years. They always represent a positive number; therefore, the effect of their compounding is also always positive. Historically, dividends have accounted for 2 percent to 4 percent of the stock market's annual return. However, this changed dramatically in the mid- to late-1990s. During that time, dividend yields dropped to all-time lows, representing approximately 1.5 percent to 1.75 percent of total return. While this is not insignificant, the fact that dividend yields are lower than they have been in the past may mean that they will not have the long-term impact on overall market performance as they once did.

Despite this, it is still important for the practitioner to understand—and make clear to prospects and clients—that this is a significant characteristic of equity indexed annuities. The purchase of an EIA that is linked to the S&P 500 is not the same as investing directly in the stocks that compose the S&P 500; the return will not be equivalent. However, this does not condemn equity indexed annuities to an inferior status. Simply stated, dividends are one of the things a buyer gives up in exchange for the elimination of market risk and the safety of having funds invested in an EIA.

Standard & Poor's does calculate separately a total return index that includes dividend reinvestment. It is this S&P 500 total return value that is generally used when comparing the performance of mutual funds or other investments against the S&P 500. If a publication of an index does include dividends, it should so state. Otherwise, dividends are not included, and so far only one or two EIAs on the market today have been designed to include dividends. The few that do include dividends have a much lower participation rate—explained below—than other designs.

■ GUARANTEED MINIMUM INTEREST RATE

The indexed interest rate notwithstanding, all equity indexed annuities—like their traditional counterparts—have a guaranteed minimum interest rate, typically 3 percent. This interest rate is mandated by insurance nonforfeiture laws. Insurance nonforfeiture laws specify the minimum values that must be paid to a contract holder upon "forfeiture" of the contract, which typically occurs when the contract is annuitized or surrendered. Historically, fixed annuities have applied the guaranteed minimum interest rate annually to the entire premium deposit. If the interest rate declared each year by the insurer is greater than 3 percent, annuity owners received this greater rate. However, the insurance company could never declare an interest rate less than 3 percent or whatever the guaranteed minimum is.

With equity indexed annuities, the guaranteed minimum interest rate is still typically 3 percent, but on many products it is applied to only 90 percent of the premium deposit. This may seem like an odd approach, but it evolved from the original annuity cash value laws that allowed a 10 percent load to cover the insurer's investment and other expenses in issuing the contract.

As you can see from Ill. 3.4, 90 percent of a $10,000 premium deposit compounding at 3 percent per year will grow back to the value of the full deposit in about three and a half years. However, in the event a contract holder surrenders the contract in the very early years, he or she could have a cash value that is less than the original deposit. Therefore, for products that use this approach (which the majority of EIAs do*), it is accurate to say that principal is guaranteed only if the contract is held for some defined period of time. Equity indexed annuities should not be sold to individuals who will have ongoing liquidity needs or who may need to surrender the contract in the very early years.

---

* Some EIA products base their minimum guarantee on 100 percent of premium deposit; it's the responsibility of the practitioner to know the mechanics of the contracts he or she sells and how they address this issue.

ILL. 3.4 ■ *Effect of the Guaranteed Interest Rate on Annuity Principal*

Annuity Premium: $10,000							
Yr. 0	Yr. 1	Yr. 2	Yr. 3	Yr. 4	Yr. 5	Yr. 6	Yr. 7
$9,000	$9,270	$9,548	$9,834	$10,129	$10,433	$10,746	$11,068
(90% of initial premium)	End-of-year values based on 3% annual compounded interest rate (rounded down to nearest dollar)						

One more important point about the guaranteed minimum rate: the values that result from the guaranteed minimum interest rate are separate from the indexed values that are produced within the contract. At the end of the contract's term, the contract holder will receive the *greater* of the guaranteed minimum value of the contract or the indexed value, as shown in Ill. 3.5.

■ SINGLE PAYMENT vs. PERIODIC PAYMENTS

The majority of equity indexed annuities on the market today accept only a single premium payment, usually $5,000 or more. However, there are some designs that will accommodate additional premium payments. In these cases, the minimum amount of additional payments the insurer will accept is typically $50 to $500. Note that participation rates (explained shortly) may differ according to the date a payment is received.

■ TERM OF CONTRACT

Virtually all EIAs are defined by an *initial accumulation term*, which varies from 1 to 15 years. Essentially, the term defines the contract's time frame since it is the length of time during which the indexed rate of return is applied to the contract; it is also the length of time that initial surrender charges (if there are any) are applied. At the end of the term, there is a window period during which the contract holder decides what he or she wants to do with the contract. At this point, the contract is fully liquid for its total value. At the end of the window, a new contract term may be started. Typically, a new term for an EIA will be similar to the original term in that indexing will resume, as will applicable surrender charges or other liquidity limits. The typical term of most equity indexed annuities on the market today is five to seven years.

ILL. 3.5 ■ *EIA Interest Crediting: Greater of Guaranteed Minimum Value or Indexed Value*

Contract holder receives greater of:

Value of Contract Based on Guaranteed Minimum Rate (3%)

Yr. 0	Yr. 1	Yr. 2	Yr. 3	Yr. 4	Yr. 5	Yr. 6	Yr. 7
$9,000	$9,270	$9,548	$9,834	$10,129	$10,433	$10,746	$11,068

(90% of initial premium)   End-of-year values based on 3% annual compounded interest rate (rounded down to nearest dollar)

Or

Value of Contract Based on Indexed Rate

Yr. 0	Yr. 1	Yr. 2	Yr. 3	Yr. 4	Yr. 5	Yr. 6	Yr. 7
$10,000	$10,480	$10,480*	$12,216	$15,540	$15,540*	$16,221	$17,437

* Index declines—no interest lost or gained; account value remains the same.

Though guaranteed minimum interest rates may be applied to only 90 percent of the original premium amount, index-linked interest is applied to 100 percent of the premium amount.

Window Periods

The *window period* for most EIAs is typically 30 to 45 days at the end of the original term and any subsequent terms. During the window period the contract holder is given the choice of what he or she wants to do with the annuity and its values. Typical options available during the window include annuitization, full or partial withdrawal of the funds or renewal of the contract for another term. Most insurers notify their contract holders of the approaching window. If the contract holder makes no choice, some insurers automatically renew the client's contract for the same length of term that was just completed. Others may automatically transfer the client's funds into an annuity with a declared annual interest rate not linked to an index. The practitioner should become familiar with the procedures of the company with whom he or she is doing business.

ILL. 3.6 ■ *EIA Participation Rates*

Contract Year	Index Yield (%)*		Participation Rate (%)		Interest Rate Applied to Contract (%)
1	8.76	×	75	=	6.57
2	12.42	×	70	=	8.69
3	6.21	×	75	=	4.66
4	− 8.76	×	75	=	0.00
5	4.11	×	80	=	3.29
6	15.61	×	65	=	10.15
7	20.21	×	80	=	16.17

* Determined by the formula the insurer uses to measure changes in the index. Though many contracts maintain the same participation rate for the contract's term, others provide for a rate that is subject to change each year, as shown above.

■ PARTICIPATION RATES

Critical to the design and function of an equity indexed annuity is the *participation rate*. The participation rate is the factor—expressed as a percentage—that converts the performance of the index to the amount of interest that will be credited to the contract. Essentially, it defines the extent to which a contract "participates" in the index return. This means that the interest-crediting process for an EIA is two-step in nature.

The first step is to determine the yield of the index itself. This is accomplished by a formula that the insurer utilizes for the product in question. Once the yield of the index is determined, the participation rate comes into play. The index yield is multiplied by the participation rate to determine the amount of interest to be credited. To use a simple example, if the S&P 500 Index rose 10 percent in a year and a contract's participation rate is 75 percent, the interest rate applied to the contract for that year would be 7.50 percent (.10 × .75). Illustration 3.6 reflects the mechanics of this process.

Participation rates can range from as low as 20 percent to over 100 percent. The value of the participation rate depends upon several things:

1. the features of the product;

2. the cost of the hedging strategy the carrier uses to back the product; and

3. the formula or methodology the carrier uses to measure changes in the index.

ILL. 3.7 ■ *EIA Margin Rate*

17.00%*	S&P 500 Index Yield
− 5.00%	Margin
12.00%	Interest Rate

* Determined by the formula the insurer uses to measure changes in the index.

A higher participation rate does not necessarily result in higher interest crediting or in a better product offering, as will be explained in Chapter 4. It is just one of many variables that should be examined when evaluating an equity indexed product.

Most EIA contracts guarantee that the participation rate will not change for the initial term of the contract, whether that is five years, seven years or some other period. Other contracts provide that the participation rate is subject to change on an annual basis.

■ MARGINS

The margin, or "spread," is another way to determine the interest rate that is applied to an EIA. Unlike a participation rate, which is *multiplied* by the index yield, a margin is *subtracted* from the index yield. For example, if the index yield is determined to be 17 percent and the margin is set at 5 percent, the interest rate applied to the annuity will be 12 percent. (See Ill. 3.7.)

A common question is: "Which is better for the client—a margin or a participation rate?" Though they represent two entirely different methods of determining an interest rate, there is a tendency to want to measure them on an "apples to apples" basis. There are various mathematical formulas and assumptions that might be used to do this, but the results would still yield an inexact approximation. A general guideline is when index returns are high, margins may produce better interest crediting. When index returns are low, participation rates may produce better interest crediting. Why? Assuming high index returns, the use of a participation rate "multiplies away" more of the return than the subtraction of a margin would. Conversely, in a low index return environment, a margin "subtracts away" more of the return than the application of a participation rate would.

■ CAPS

Some EIA designs contain a feature known as a *cap*. A cap is a limit on the amount of indexed-linked interest credited to the annuity in a given time period, regardless of what the participation rate or margin produces. For instance, a product with a

ILL. 3.8 ■ *EIA Floor*

Index yield as determined by formula	Yr. 1	Yr. 2	Yr. 3	Yr. 4	Yr. 5	Yr. 6	Yr. 7
	10%	2%	− 18%	6%	4%	8%	7%
Interest credited*	7%	1.4%	0%	4.2%	2.8%	5.6%	4.9%

No interest credited due to negative index value; account value remains the same.

* Assumes 70 percent participation rate.

14 percent annual cap will limit the yearly interest earned to 14 percent. Another product might limit the interest credited over the contract's initial term to 100 percent of the premium deposit. With some contracts, the cap amount can change annually. Others guarantee the cap for the entire initial term of the contract.

Caps may appear to be a substantial drawback, especially in years when the index increases substantially. However, it's important to understand that, because the insurer is protected against very substantial index increases, it is able to provide other attractive product features. Without the cap, these features could never be offered.

■ FLOOR

Also common to some EIA designs is a *floor* on the amount of interest credited. In this context, the floor is the minimum amount of index-linked interest that will be credited to a contract in any one year or over a multiple of years. It is a feature that applies to contracts that calculate and credit index interest on an annual or multi-year basis. In most contracts that contain this feature, the floor is 0 percent, meaning that there will be no interest credited if the index declines. However, the client's account value will not suffer a loss; it remains the same as the previous year. For example, let's assume in a given year the value of the S&P 500 experienced a −20 percent return. This does not translate into a −20 percent interest credit for the client; instead, the floor provides for 0 percent interest. Illustration 3.8 shows how the floor comes into play on an equity indexed annuity.

An equity indexed annuity's floor should not be confused with its guaranteed minimum interest rate. The minimum interest rate, as we have learned, is typically 3 percent on 90 percent of premium, compounded annually over the life of the contract. The guaranteed minimum interest rate determines the value that will be received by the client *at the end of the contract term* if the index-linked interest accumulations are less than this amount. By contrast, the floor represents the worst the client can do with respect to the amount of index-linked interest credited *in any given year* or *series of years.*

■ VESTING

Some products utilize what is known as a *vesting schedule.* "Vesting" refers to the amount of the index value credited to the contract that is available to the contract holder for withdrawals or surrenders. Effectively, vesting operates to transfer credited interest from a contract's account value to its surrender value. A typical vesting schedule might provide for 20 percent vesting at the end of the first contract year and increase by 20 percent each year thereafter, until 100 percent of the indexed-linked interest is available at the end of the fifth year. For example, let's say that $10,000 is invested in an EIA that contains a 20 percent per year vesting schedule. The contract's value grows as follows:

	Beginning Year Account Value		Interest Credited		End-of-Year Account Value
Year 1	$10,000	+	$1,500	=	$11,500
Year 2	$11,500	+	$1,150	=	$12,650
Year 3	$12,650	+	$ 0	=	$12,650
Year 4	$12,650	+	$ 950	=	$13,600
Year 5	$13,600	+	$1,600	=	$15,200

The vesting schedule would produce the following:

	Interest Credited (Cumulative)		Percentage of Interest Vested		Amount of Interest Vested
Year 1	$1,500	×	20%	=	$ 300
Year 2	$2,650	×	40%	=	$1,060
Year 3	$2,650	×	60%	=	$1,590
Year 4	$3,600	×	80%	=	$2,880
Year 5	$5,200	×	100%	=	$5,200

As you can see, by the end of the fifth contract year, the owner is fully vested in the interest that has been credited to the contract.

The purpose of a vesting schedule is to protect the insurer against early contract surrenders. By limiting the amount of the index interest that is available for withdrawals and surrenders, the insurer discourages early surrenders. An insurance company may require the protection of a vesting schedule because it has purchased financial instruments to back the product that will cover the entire term of the contract (typically five to seven years). Contract holders who surrender their contracts prematurely could force the carrier to unwind some of these investments.

■ LIQUIDITY

Liquidity—the owner's ability to access his or her funds without cost or penalty prior to the end of the surrender charge period—is often an issue with annuities. It is no different with EIAs. However, because the design of EIAs can be very different from other fixed annuities, the liquidity options may also vary. Most traditional fixed annuities provide for an annual "free withdrawal," which allows the owner to withdraw up to 10 percent of the contract's accumulated value each year without incurring a surrender charge. More than half of the EIAs on the market today provide for a 10 percent (or other) free withdrawal of indexed values. Other designs may provide for a free withdrawal from the contract's guaranteed minimum values or from the vested values, as described above.

Many EIAs also contain a provision that allows withdrawal of contract values in the event the owner is confined to a nursing home or is diagnosed with a terminal illness. It is important that the practitioner evaluate closely any potential product offering to determine its liquidity terms. However, as a general rule of thumb, it's fair to say that equity indexed annuities are not typically designed to address ongoing liquidity needs during the initial or any subsequent term.

■ DEATH BENEFIT

An important feature of all annuities is the *death benefit*. It is one of the benefits that distinguishes annuities from other savings and investment products. The death benefit is the amount of contract value paid directly to the beneficiary upon the death of the owner, usually expressed as the amount of premium paid (less any withdrawals), or the contract's accumulated value, if greater. Values that are paid out due to the death of the owner are usually not subject to surrender charges. If a spouse is the primary beneficiary of the contract, he or she may opt to keep the contract in force, continuing its tax-deferred status.

As it applies to an equity indexed annuity, the death benefit may operate a bit differently. With some EIA designs, indexed interest may not be available until the end of the term. Consequently, the death of a contract holder prior to the end of the term presents some unique challenges. Various product designs address this challenge in different ways; for example, the death benefit value may include some calculated level of interest that has been earned through a particular point in time, such as a prior contract anniversary date. In all cases, however, there is a provision for a minimum death benefit, which is equivalent to the guaranteed minimum value of the contract, usually without assessment of any surrender charges. The practitioner should be familiar with the death benefit provisions of the contract he or she is representing.

■ SURRENDER CHARGES

EIAs may differ from other fixed annuities when it comes to *surrender charges*. Though some EIAs, like their traditional counterparts, have an explicit surrender charge schedule that declines over the number of years the contract is held, others have no explicit surrender charges at all. Instead, they might limit the owner's ability to access credited interest through a vesting process, as described, or they may offer interim access only to guaranteed minimum contract values.

It is important to note that the absence of explicit surrender charges does not mean that it is inexpensive to surrender one of these products. In some cases, a contract holder could lose all of the previously earned indexed interest if the contract is surrendered early. If the amount of interest is substantial, it is obviously more expensive to lose interest than it would be to incur charges assessed under a typical surrender charge schedule.

■ ANNUITIZATION

Annuitization is an important feature of annuities. Consumers are becoming ever more aware of the personal responsibility they have to secure their retirement. As the Baby Boom generation ages, the billions of dollars that are being saved for retirement will eventually need to be converted into an income stream to help supplement other sources of retirement income such as Social Security and pension benefits. For these individuals—and for the many who are now at retirement's front door—annuitization is the only way to produce a steady income flow that is guaranteed to last a lifetime.

Though the accumulation of funds within an equity indexed annuity operates differently than a traditional declared-rate annuity, the annuitization of those funds operates in exactly the same way. Once the values are annuitized, the income stream is fixed; the monthly payments will not vary. The insurance company assumes an annuitization rate of interest that takes into account the client's age and sex, the length of time the money will be paid out and whether the payment is based on a single life or a joint life.

Some insurers have been exploring how to link the monthly annuity payments to the performance of the S&P 500 in some way. It is possible in the future that there will be a number of equity indexed annuities (both deferred and immediate) that will offer such a feature.

■ SUMMARY

This chapter examined the features of equity indexed annuities, including indexing, participation rates, margins, windows, caps, floors and vesting—terms that define the unique characteristics of EIAs. It is critical for the practitioner to review the terms and provisions of the contracts he or she sells so that these features are fully understood and can be clearly explained to prospects and clients. In the next chapter, we delve deeper into these products by examining various EIA designs and the ways in which indexed returns are determined and credited.

■ CHAPTER REVIEW QUESTIONS

1. The index to which most EIAs link their interest rate is the

   A. S&P 100 Index
   B. Dow Jones Industrial Average Index
   C. S&P 500 Index
   D. New York Stock Exchange Composite Index

2. An investment in an EIA that is linked to a price index is the same as investing directly in the stocks that comprise the index.

   True or False

3. An amount typically equal to 3 percent on 90 percent of the premium deposit defines what EIA feature?

   A. Surrender charge
   B. Death benefit, if the contract owner dies prior to the end of the term
   C. Floor on the credited index yield
   D. Minimum guaranteed interest rate

4. If the index yield is 10 percent and the interest rate applied to an EIA contract is 7.5 percent, what is the participation rate?

   A. 2.5 percent
   B. 7.5 percent
   C. 25 percent
   D. 75 percent

5. A newly purchased EIA contract contains the following features: a 90 percent participation rate; a 14 percent cap; a 0 percent floor; and a 20 percent per year vesting schedule. During the first year, the indexed interest yield was determined to be 16 percent. What will be credited to the contract for that year?

   A. 3.2 percent
   B. 14 percent
   C. 14.4 percent
   D. 16 percent

4

Indexing Methodolgies

W hat most practitioners know about indexing of financial products is based on indexed mutual funds. Unfortunately, this does not translate well into an understanding of indexing methodologies for fixed annuities. Whereas there is only one indexing method used for mutual funds—the fund purchases stocks that compose the index—the methodologies applied to annuities are limited only by the creativity of the financial services communities. In other words, there are no limits.

There is probably nothing more important to the overall performance of an EIA and its suitability for a buyer than its indexing methodology. For that reason, it is vital that the practitioner understand how the products he or she sells operate. In this chapter, we will explore six different indexing methods currently being used by EIA carriers.

■ ■ ■ ■ ■

■ INDEXING METHODS

The defining feature of an equity indexed annuity product is the way in which its interest rate is determined and credited. This is the basis of the product's design and it is determined by the way in which the insurer calculates the gain in the index to which the product is linked. There are a number of different methodologies that are currently being used; in fact, the method used gives the product its name. Though there are many variations, six distinct methodologies have emerged as the most common: point-to-point; high water mark; annual reset; low water mark; multi-year reset; and digital. Inherent to each are certain features that further refine how the indexed rate of return is applied. These include floors, participation rates or margins, averaging and caps.

As you will see, each design has benefits and drawbacks.

■ POINT-TO-POINT METHOD

The *point-to-point* (PTP) product design represents the simplest and most straight-forward method of applying an indexed rate of return to an EIA. Also known as the *end-point* method, the name fairly describes the methodology. The value of the index to which the product is linked is marked at two points: a beginning point and an end point. The beginning point is the day the contract holder's premium is deposited in the contract (or otherwise credited to the contract), which starts the indexing period. The end point is the last day of the contract's initial term. The difference in the index value between the beginning point and the end point is the basis for the amount of interest that will be credited to the annuity. It is a simple calculation to determine the index return for that period:

$$\frac{EP - BP}{BP}$$

where EP is the end point value of the index and BP is the beginning point value of the index.

To this, the participation rate (or margin) is applied and the result is the amount of interest credited to the contract. Let's look at a very simple example.

Assume the S&P 500 Index is at 1000 when Stan deposits $20,000 in an equity indexed annuity. The contract has an initial term of seven years, uses point-to-point interest crediting and provides for 100 percent participation. Seven years later, at the end of the initial term, the index is at 1500. The gain in the index over the term is 50 percent ([1500 – 1000] ÷ 1000). Because the participation rate on Stan's contract is 100 percent, the full 50 percent of the index return will be applied, resulting in $10,000 of credited interest.

Now, what would happen if, instead of registering a gain, the value of the index declined over the term of Stan's contract? Let's assume that at the end of the initial term, the index is at 800, which would equate to a 20 percent decline ([800 – 1000] ÷ 1000). What effect does this have on the interest credited to Stan's contract? In this case, the minimum guaranteed rate would be applied. With an equity indexed annuity—no matter what methodology is used—the contract holder is protected against loss; the amount credited to the contract is the greater of the amount the indexing formula produces or the guaranteed minimum. If the provisions of Stan's contract are typical, this minimum would be 3 percent, credited to 90 percent of his deposit, and compounded annually over the term. This would translate into $4,138 of credited interest (3 percent of $18,000 compounded over seven years) for a net gain of $2,138 on the original $20,000 deposit.

How the PTP Method Works

One of the advantages of the point-to-point method is its simplicity. It operates the way people understand an equity-oriented investment operates: there is the start point (the day the contract is purchased and the premium is deposited) and there is the end point (the last day of the contract's term). Quite simply, the difference in the value of the index between those two points defines the index gain—or loss—which, in turn, drives the interest rate applied to the contract. For purposes of calculating the change in index value, what happens between these two points is irrelevant. However, to fully appreciate the PTP method, one has to understand that the way the market performs during the two points does have a critical effect on the amount of interest that will be credited to the contract.

To illustrate this concept, let's return to our example. In the first instance, we said that the S&P 500 was at 1000 when Stan purchased his seven-year PTP contract and it was at 1500 at the end of the contract's initial term. Let's assume that the market's performance during this period was as follows:

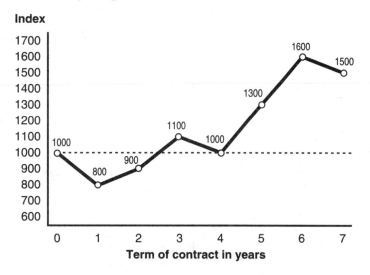

Again, the index return over the contract's term is a simple calculation based on the value of the index at the contract's beginning point and at its end point ([1500 − 1000] ÷ 1000). But the simplicity of the calculation belies the impact of market movement. Though we might say that what happens between the beginning point and the end point is irrelevant, what happens between these points does affect where the index value winds up. For example, let's assume that the index did not drop during the first year of the contract as shown above; instead, it remained level and then experienced the same gains as shown above in years two through seven. The result is an end point that is 200 points higher:

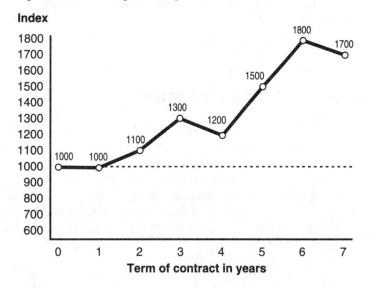

Consequently, instead of a 50 percent return, Stan's contract would be credited with a 70 percent return ([1700 − 1000] ÷ 1000), resulting in $14,000 of interest.

The PTP method is simple and straightforward and produces good results in bullish market environments. But it is also very dependent on a single end-point. Years of index gains over a contract's term can be wiped out by a little bad timing at the end. Of course, the contract owner is always protected against loss by the guaranteed minimum rate, but the risk of not participating in any positive movement the market experienced over the contract's term exists.

Second, PTP products lack what is best described as "instant gratification." This results from the way in which the index return is calculated. For example, assume Sally is one year into a seven-year PTP contract and the S&P 500 has just experienced a 25 percent gain. How does she determine the extent to which that 25 percent gain will affect where the index will be when her contract term is over? She can't. The market may trend down from that point over the next six years or it may continue to rise. The point is, Sally will not know whether any part of that 25 percent gain will be hers to keep until the end of the seventh year when the contract matures.

Through various product design provisions, the effects of these drawbacks can be mitigated. For one thing, the one-day dependency problem can be handled with an *averaging technique*, which serves to "smooth out" peaks and valleys in the movement of the index. (This is discussed more fully later in the chapter.) The lack of instant gratification problem can be managed through a *vesting schedule*, as previously explained. Vesting in a PTP product means that some portion of the cumulative gain the index experiences at each anniversary date is credited to the contract, subject to participation rates and surrender charges. In the example above, if Sally's contract contained a vesting schedule that provided for 20 percent vesting in the first year, then 20 percent of the 25 percent gain (i.e., 5 percent) would be credited as "hers to keep" interest (assuming 100 percent participation).

When PTP Works Best

A point-to-point product works best in a very bullish market environment. As a general rule, these products have high participation rates, relative to other product designs. They will not be strong performers in a market that is highly volatile but does not trend up over the term. Approximately one-third of EIAs on the market today use the PTP method.

■ HIGH WATER MARK METHOD

The *high water mark* (HWM) method of crediting interest is another popular design. It too uses two points to calculate the index return. The beginning point is the day the premium is deposited in the contract. The end point—for purposes of the calculation—is not an end point in time but the point at which the value of the index reached its highest point, as marked by contract anniversary dates. In a seven-year term contract, for instance, the end point would be the highest of the index values on each of the seven anniversary dates. The index yield is determined by the difference between the value of the index as of the beginning point and the value of the index as of the high water end point:

$$\frac{HP - BP}{BP}$$

where HP is the high point value of the index and BP is the beginning point value of the index.

In every other way, the mechanics of the high water mark method are the same as the point-to-point method.

How the HWM Method Works

To illustrate the high water mark methodology, let's assume that the S&P 500 was at 1000 when Iris invested $50,000 in a HWM equity indexed annuity. The contract has an initial term of seven years and a 90 percent participation rate. As marked by the anniversary dates of her contract, these were the index values:

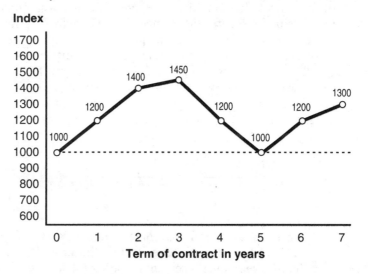

For Iris, the high point would be marked by the contract's third anniversary date, where the indexed value reached 1450. For purposes of the calculation, this point effectively becomes the end point and the value as of that date determines the yield for the contract's entire term. Thus, the index yield for the contract's term would be 45 percent ([1450 – 1000] ÷ 1000). To this, the participation rate of 90 percent is applied. The result is a 40.5 percent rate of return credited to Iris's contract, or $20,250.

The high water mark method is not plagued by some of the disadvantages inherent to the point-to-point method. Specifically, it does provide some instant gratification in that the contract holder knows that a high water mark has been locked in when he or she reaches that point. In addition, because this mark has been locked in, any late term decline in the index will not have the same negative effect that it would under a PTP formula. On the other hand, because most products using the HWM method measure the high water mark at contract year-ends, the owner is limited to those singular days for his or her results. In addition, a HWM product usually has a lower participation rate than a PTP product. (This is due to the cost to the insurer of investing for HWM designs, which will be explored in Chapter 5.)

When the HWM Method Works Best

The high water mark methodology works well in a number of different financial environments, but compared to other product designs, it will be the best performer in a market that peaks early during a given term and then declines for the remainder of the term. Compared to an annual reset product (discussed next), a HWM design will perform poorly in a highly volatile market that does not achieve a very high point along the way.

■ ANNUAL RESET METHOD

The *annual reset* method of calculating an indexed return is sometimes called the "annual ratchet" (or simply, "ratchet") method. It operates very differently from the high water mark and point-to-point methods. Instead of evaluating the performance of the index with a singular beginning point and a singular end point, the annual reset method measures the changes in the index with a *series* of beginning points and end points. These beginning points and end points usually correspond to the beginning and end of each contract year. The performance of the index stands on its own—and is measured—each and every year. In effect, at each policy anniversary date, the beginning point is "reset" and the yield, up or down, for the following year is based on the index's performance from that reset point. The formula for calculating the return of the index using an annual reset method would look like this:

$$\left[\frac{EP_{Yr\,1} - BP_{Yr\,1}}{BP_{Yr\,1}}\right] + \left[\frac{EP_{Yr\,2} - BP_{Yr\,2}}{BP_{Yr\,2}}\right] + \dots \left[\frac{EP_{Yr\,n} - BP_{Yr\,n}}{BP_{Yr\,n}}\right]$$

where EP is the end point index value, BP is the beginning point index value and n is the number of years in the term. If EP minus BP is negative for any year, then 0 percent is used for that year.

How the Annual Reset Design Works

Putting this design into context, let's say that Lou invested $75,000 in an annual reset EIA. The contract has a 5-year initial term and a 70 percent participation rate, guaranteed for the term. Over the term of Lou's contract, the values of the S&P 500 (as marked by contract anniversary dates) were as follows:

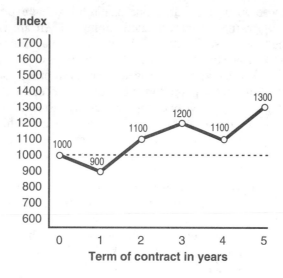

Index

Term of contract in years

The conversion of the index values into the interest to be credited to Lou's contract would be done annually:

	Yr. 1	*Yr. 2*	*Yr. 3*	*Yr. 4*	*Yr. 5*
S&P 500 gain:	0 +	$\dfrac{1100 - 900}{900}$ +	$\dfrac{1200 - 1100}{1100}$ +	0 +	$\dfrac{1300 - 1100}{1100}$
Participation rate applied:	0 +	$.222 \times .70$ +	$.091 \times .70$ +	0 +	$.182 \times .70$
Amount of interest credited:	0 +	$11,655 +	$4,778 +	0 +	$9,555 = $25,988*

The methodology of an annual reset design can yield powerful results. In years when the index is up, the contract holder participates in the upward direction (subject to the participation rate or margin). If the index is down for a given year, the typical result is a zero interest credit for that year. This is how the "floor" comes into play. Most annual reset products have a floor of zero that applies in any given year, meaning that an annual yield never drops below zero. This is not the only advantage, however. In addition to being "out" in a down year, the contract holder also has the benefit of starting over the next year at the lower index value. Historically, some of the best years in the stock market occur on the heels of some of the worst years. In this way, an annual reset EIA offers some of the advantages of perfect market timing: the contract holder is "in" for the good times and "out" for the bad.

---

* The formula and example that illustrate how the annual reset method works show simple, or additive, interest. Some annual reset products use compound interest. The trade-offs of using one approach as opposed to the other are explained later in this chapter.

Given these positive features, one would think that every equity indexed annuity would employ the annual reset methodology. There are a couple of reasons why this is not the case. First, this approach runs somewhat counter to conventional thought as to how an investment works, in that it operates on an annual basis but the contract itself extends over a number of years. For both practitioner and consumer, this requires additional explanation and training. Second, and more importantly, an annual reset design is very expensive for the insurer. The cost of administering annual reset contracts and investing for them is much higher than with other types of EIA designs. Consequently, all other factors being equal, the annual reset design usually has the lowest participation rate of all EIA designs.

Another point one must consider with an annual reset design is whether or not the interest credited to the contract is compounded. Since returns are calculated on a year-to-year basis, it is possible to incorporate compounding of interest into the product's design and, certainly, this is something that most contract holders would desire. For example, if the provisions of Lou's contract included annual compounding of interest (and all other factors were the same), the amount credited to his contract over the initial term would be an additional $2,930:

	Yr. 1	Yr. 2	Yr. 3	Yr. 4	Yr. 5	Total
Interest credited without compounding:	0	$11,655	$4,778	0	$9,555	$25,988
Interest credited with compounding:	0	$11,655	$5,520	0	$11,743	$28,918

Since the annual reset methodology is so expensive, one way insurers can keep cost levels reasonable is not to include a compounding feature. On the other hand, if compounding is included in the product's design, it is likely the product will contain a *cap*, which limits the amount of interest that will be credited in any interest-crediting period, regardless of the participation rate. The inclusion or omission of a compounding feature is simply one more thing that needs to be evaluated when an individual is considering the purchase of an EIA contract.

When the Annual Reset Design Works Best

Annual reset products work best in a market that is highly volatile over the term. Again, the contract holder participates in market uptrends and, due to the floor, is "out" when the market trends down. Compared to other product designs, annual resets perform the worst in a steadily rising market with low volatility.

■ LOW WATER MARK METHOD

Contrary to what its name implies, the *low water mark* (LWM) product design can produce significant yields. With this method, the end point is the last day of the term; the beginning point is marked by the contract anniversary date when the index reached its lowest value. The formula for calculating the percentage gain in the index using this methodology is:

$$\frac{EP - LP}{LP}$$

where EP is the end point value of the index and LP is the low point value of the index.

How the LWM Method Works

Let's say Bud invests $50,000 in an equity indexed annuity that uses a low water mark methodology. It is a seven-year initial term contract with a 95 percent participation rate. Over the term of Bud's contract, the S&P 500 performs as follows:

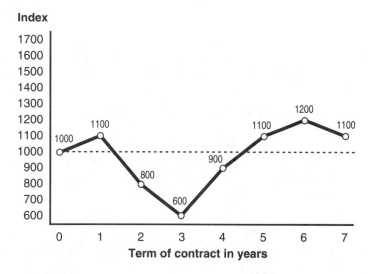

For purposes of calculating the index return, the end point would be the end of the contract term when the index is at 1100; the low point would be marked by the contract's third anniversary date, when the S&P 500 reached 600. This would calculate into a return of 83.3 percent for the index ([1100 – 600] ÷ 600). Applying the participation rate, this would produce a return of 79.1 (83.3 × .95) percent for Bud's contract, or $39,550.

When the LWM Design Works Best

By using a low water mark as the start point, a LWM product offers the opportunity for significant results. The lower the start point, the higher the resultant index return. Though it works well in a number of different market environments, it will perform the best in a market that declines precipitously early in the contract and then rises throughout the remainder of the term. It will not perform well in a market that declines early and stays down.

■ MULTI-YEAR RESET METHOD

A *multi-year reset* method operates very much like an annual reset method with one key difference: instead of looking at the results of the index one year at a time, this approach measures the results of the index over multiple years. At the end of the multiple-year period, a new beginning point is reset and another multiple-year period begins. The number of years to reset is always less than the length of the initial term. A typical multi-year reset will calculate the index return every two to three years. The formula for calculating the performance of the index using a multi-year reset methodology is:

$$\left[\frac{EP_{RP\,1} - BP_{RP\,0}}{BP_{RP\,0}}\right] + \left[\frac{EP_{RP\,2} - BP_{RP\,1}}{BP_{RP\,1}}\right] + \cdots\cdots \left[\frac{EP_{RP\,n} - BP_{RP\,n-1}}{BP_{RP\,n-1}}\right]$$

where EP equals the end point index value, BP equals the beginning point index value, *RP* is the reset period, and *n* is the number of reset periods in the term. If EP minus BP is less than zero in any given period, then 0 percent is used for that period.

How the Multi-Year Reset Method Works

Let's assume Pat invests $45,000 in a multi-year reset EIA. The product has a six-year initial term with resets every two years and a participation rate of 90 percent. The S&P 500 was at 1000 when Pat purchased the product; over the term of the contract, the index performed as follows:

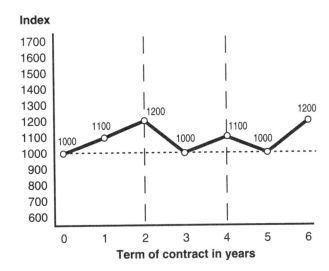

For purposes of determining the interest to be credited to Pat's contract, each of the three periods is treated separately. This would result in three interest calculations:

	First Period *(Years 1 and 2)*		*Second Period* *(Years 3 and 4)*		*Third Period* *(Years 5 and 6)*
S&P 500 performance:	$\dfrac{1200 - 1000}{1000}$	$+$	$\dfrac{1100 - 1200}{1200}$	$+$	$\dfrac{1200 - 1100}{1100}$
Interest:	.20	$+$	0 (floor applies)	$+$	.091

Applying the participation rate (and assuming that the contract provides for simple interest), Pat would be credited with $11,790 in interest earnings for the entire contract term.

A multi-year reset annuity is a cross between a point-to-point and an annual reset design. Whereas the indexing calculation period in a point-to-point product is exactly the same length as the initial term, at which time the contract can be renewed and a beginning point reset from the end of the initial term, the number of years to reset in a multi-year product is always less than the length of the initial term. If the performance of the index is positive during any multi-year period (two years in the above example), the participation rate is applied to determine interest earnings. If the performance of the index is negative during any multi-year period, no interest is credited (but none is lost either). The results of the multi-year periods are either added together (if the contract provides for simple interest) or they are multiplied together (if the contract provides for compound interest) to determine the total end-of-term interest.

When the Multi-Year Reset Design Works Best

Multi-year reset products perform well in a moderately volatile market, especially if the peaks and valleys of the market's performance coincide with the product's reset points. Compared to other EIA designs, it works the worst in a steadily rising market with low volatility.

■ DIGITAL METHOD

The *digital method* is known for its simplicity. Based on an "ON / OFF" principle, it credits a specified rate of return each year the index return is positive and another specified rate of return—typically 0 percent—each year the index return is negative. For example, a digital contract might credit a 10 percent interest rate for each year the index shows a positive return and 0 percent for each year the index return is zero or negative. In this way, digital contracts are credited annually with one of two rates of interest. In this example, our contract would credit each year either 10 percent ("ON") or 0 percent ("OFF"). Normally, the specified rates apply for the duration of the contract's initial term; they are not usually subject to change.

How the Digital Method Works

The formula for calculating the percentage gain in the index using the digital method is very simple:

$$\text{If } EP_n - BP_n \text{ is positive, add } X\% \text{ interest}$$

$$\text{If } EP_n - BP_n \text{ is negative, add } 0\% \text{ interest}$$

where EP is the end point index value, BP is the beginning point index value and n is equal to each year in the contract's initial term.

Let's say Linda deposits $60,000 in a digital EIA. The contract provides for a credit of 10 percent interest each year the performance of the S&P 500 is positive and 0 percent each year the performance is flat or negative. It is a seven-year contract with 100 percent participation. Over the term of her contract, the S&P 500 performed as shown:

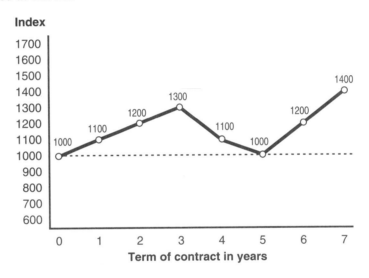

The digital approach assesses the performance of the index one year at a time. Accordingly, the interest crediting to Linda's contract would be as follows:

	Yr. 1	*Yr. 2*	*Yr. 3*	*Yr. 4*	*Yr. 5*	*Yr. 6*	*Yr. 7*
S&P 500 Performance:	+10%	+9.1%	+8.3%	−15.4%	−9.1%	+20%	+16.6%
Interest Credited:	.10	.10	.10	0	0	.10	.10

Assuming Linda's contract provided for simple interest, she would be credited with $30,000 in interest for the entire term.

Like the annual reset method, a digital contract evaluates the performance of the index one year at a time. However, whereas the annual reset method provides the opportunity for the contract to receive substantial upside in the year following a big downside, the digital method limits the upside potential to whatever the digitized interest growth is. Another point to evaluate when one is considering a digital contract is whether or not interest is compounded, since the design can provide for either. A digital contract that does not offer compound interest crediting may, as a trade-off, offer a higher rate of interest when the index has a positive return.

When the Digital Method Works Best

Digital product designs work best in a market that rises slightly each year. Compared to other EIA designs, they work the worst in a market that alternates downturns with large upswings, especially if the downturns are small.

■ OTHER EIA DESIGN FEATURES

The preceding discussion focused on specific EIA designs which, as we saw, are defined primarily by the method that is used to measure the performance of the index to which the product is tied. To these basic designs are commonly included features that further define how—or to what extent—a given contract will be credited with the index's return. A contract *floor* is one example. The *participation rate* or *margin* is another. Additionally, there is *averaging* and *caps*.

Floors

EIA contracts that calculate and apply the index return over periods that are shorter than the full term of the contract typically contain a provision for a *floor*. The floor represents the minimum amount of the index return that will be credited for any given calculation period. For most products that contain this feature, the floor is zero. Thus, if the index return for any given period is negative, the amount of interest applied for that period is zero. This means that the contract's account value will never decline due to a decrease in the value of the index. An annual reset product would typically contain a floor; a point-to-point product would not. A multi-year reset product would likely contain a floor; a high water mark product would not.

Again, it is worth making the distinction between the floor and the guaranteed minimum rate of return. All EIA contracts contain a guaranteed minimum rate of return; it represents the *required* amount of interest that will be applied to the contract at the end of its term. By contrast, the floor is the minimum amount of *index-linked* interest that will be applied to a contract in any given period. At the end of the contract's term, the *greater* of the required minimum rate of return or the index-linked rate of return is credited to the contract.

Participation Rate vs. Margin

The difference between participation rates and margins was described in Chapter 3. Throughout this chapter, we used examples of products that had participation rates since the preponderance of EIA contracts on the market today employ participation rates instead of margins. Only a small number of products use a margin methodology. Margins may be used for any EIA design but are most common to annual reset products.

Using a margin instead of a participation rate does not alter the product's underlying methodology or its consequent advantages and disadvantages. It will, however, alter the amount of interest credited to the annuity. When compared to a

---

ILL. 4.1 ■ *Comparing Methodologies: Participation Rate vs. Margin*

Compare: Annual reset product with 5 percent margin

Annual reset product with 60 percent participation rate

Scenario 1: High Index Return for the Year

	Participation Rate Method	Margin Method
Index return	30%	30%
Multiply participation rate *or* subtract margin	× 60%	– 5%
Interest credited	18%	25%

Scenario 2: Low Index Return for the Year

	Participation Rate Method	Margin Method
Index return	5%	5%
Multiply participation rate *or* subtract margin	× 60%	– 5%
Interest credited	3%	0%

---

participation rate, use of a margin tends to increase interest credited in years that produce high index returns and to decrease interest credited in years that are marked by low index returns. Illustration 4.1 shows these results.

Averaging

Many practitioners make the mistake of thinking that *averaging* is a method of calculating index returns when, instead, it is a feature that many indexing methods incorporate. For purposes of calculating an index return, averaging removes the dependence on a single day as a beginning point or an end point.

Averaging takes the closing index prices over a certain number of days, adds them up and then divides by the same number of days, which results in an overall averaged point. (Averaging can also be done using months or quarters.) An averaged point may be either an end point or a beginning point, though most often it is an end point. The most common use of averaging is in the final year of a point-to-point product. Again, it serves to reduce the influence of or dependency on the final day of the term. Let's look at an example.

Assume Neil invests $75,000 in a seven-year point-to-point annuity with 100 percent participation. The S&P 500 is at 1000 when he purchases the product. Over the course of the contract's initial term, the S&P 500 performs as follows:

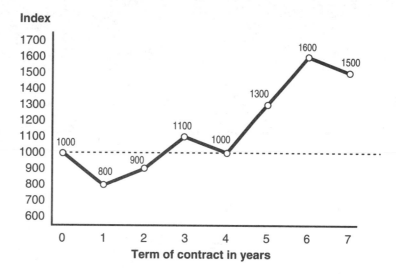

Without an averaging feature, the index return for Neil's contract would be computed with 1500 as the end point, resulting in a 50 percent return ([1500 − 1000] ÷ 1000).

Now let's say that Neil's contract did include an averaging feature, which averages the S&P 500 closing prices for the last year's four quarters. Here's how that final year looked:

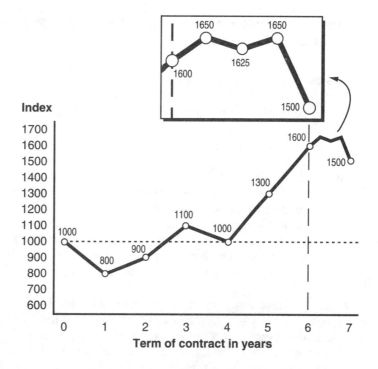

ILL. 4.2 ■ *S&P 500, 1987 and 1995*

Year	Index Start Point	Index End Point	Daily Averaged End Point	Nonaveraged Index Return	Averaged Index Return
1987	242.17	247.08	286.97	2.03%	18.50%
1995	459.27	615.93	541.71	34.11%	17.95%

For purposes of calculating the index return, the end point would be the average of the S&P 500's closing prices as of each quarter in the seventh year:

$$\frac{1650 + 1625 + 1650 + 1500}{4} = 1606.25$$

Consequently, averaging would produce a 60.6 percent return for Neil's contract: $(1606.25 - 1000) \div 1000$.

Averaging is a volatility dampener. It serves to take out the peaks and valleys of the index movement and has a smoothing effect. In a year that the index climbs significantly during the majority of the year then sells off toward the end, averaging will produce excellent results. In a year that the index goes up linearly, averaging will cut the return in half. The years 1987 and 1995 exemplify these kinds of trends, as illustrated in Ill. 4.2. An averaging feature can be incorporated into any kind of index methodology.

Caps

Like averaging, a *cap* is not an indexing methodology but a feature that may be included as part of an index design. As you will recall, a cap places a ceiling on the amount of index-linked interest that will be credited to an EIA. Caps can be applied on an annual basis or over the entire term of the contract. For example, a contract might impose a cap of 18 percent every year (meaning that the amount of interest credited annually will be no more than 18 percent) or a cap of 100 percent over the initial term (meaning that the total amount of interest credited to the contract by the end of its initial term will be no more than the full amount of the premium deposit). Contracts that contain annual caps usually reserve the right to adjust the cap—up or down—each year. Though caps may be applied to any index method they are most likely to be found on annual reset products.

Caps can have a significant effect on the amount of interest credited to an equity indexed annuity but must be evaluated in light of the other features and provisions the contract contains. The inclusion of a cap should point the buyer to look for a feature that "balances" the limit imposed on interest earnings. For example, it's common for products that contain caps to compound interest earnings whereas products that do not cap interest may provide for simple interest.

■ SUMMARY

The indexing methodologies that define today's EIA products are diverse and each has benefits and drawbacks. Regardless of the method, for the practitioner, the most important part of helping clients choose the right design comes in understanding the product. If the practitioner does not understand the product, there is little chance the buyer will understand the product. Therefore, it is imperative that the practitioner knows which product designs will work best for a client and becomes educated about every detail of those offerings. This knowledge will help the client feel comfortable with his or her annuity purchase and will minimize the risk of misunderstandings or errors.

■ CHAPTER REVIEW QUESTIONS

1. The EIA product methodology that works the best in a very bullish market is

   A. point-to-point
   B. high water mark
   C. digital
   D. low water mark

2. EIA participation rates

   A. are a measure of how much stock market risk the contract holder assumes
   B. convert indexing results to contract holder interest
   C. measure how much of the contract's premium is invested in bonds
   D. are synonymous with a contract's surrender charges

3. With a high water mark EIA, which two points in the contract's term are used to calculate the index return?

   A. The point when the owner's premium is credited to the contract and the point when the index reaches its highest during the first contract year
   B. The point when the index reaches its lowest during the contract's initial term and the point when it reaches its highest
   C. The point when the contract reaches its highest during the contract's first year and the last day of the contract's term
   D. The point when the index reaches its highest during the contract's initial term and the point when the owner's premium is credited to the contract

4. Averaging should NOT be considered an indexing methodology.

   True or False

5. EIA Product *X* marks the S&P 500 at the point when the contract holder's premium is deposited in the contract and again at the end of the contract's initial term. The difference between the index values at these marks is the methodology behind the interest credited to Product *X*. Product *X* is a

   A. low-water mark product
   B. digital product
   C. point-to-point product
   D. annual reset product

6. Mark invested $10,000 in a five-year point-to-point EIA, with a 50 percent participation rate. At purchase, the S&P 500 was at 1000; five years later at the end of the contract's term, the S&P 500 was at 950. How much interest will be credited to Mark's contract?

   A. The contract's minimum guaranteed rate
   B. 0 percent
   C. – 2.5 percent
   D. – 5 percent

7. Stacy invested $20,000 in a seven-year low water mark EIA. Over the term of her contract, the S&P 500 Index, as marked by her contract anniversary dates, was as follows:

Year 1:	1200	Year 5:	1250
Year 2:	900	Year 6:	1260
Year 3:	950	Year 7:	1320
Year 4:	1100		

   What is the index yield for Stacy's contract term?

   A. 10.0 percent
   B. 25.0 percent
   C. 31.8 percent
   D. 46.7 percent

8. Which EIA indexing method credits a specified rate of return each year the index return is positive and another rate of return—typically 0—each year the index return is negative?

   A. Point-to-point
   B. Low water mark
   C. Digital
   D. Multi-year reset

5

Managing the Equity Indexed Annuity

To fully understand equity indexed products, the practitioner must understand the fundamentals of the insurer's investment strategy and the challenges it faces when investing for these unique contracts. Though all insurers do not employ the same methodology, there is enough consistency from carrier to carrier to discuss the issues in more than general terms. Understanding the investment strategy behind the EIA will help the practitioner better explain the product's features and benefits to prospects and clients.

■ ■ ■ ■ ■

■ THE INSURER'S INVESTMENT STRATEGY

To the carrier, the biggest difference between declared-rate fixed annuities and equity indexed annuities lies in the investment strategy it must employ to manage these products. The easiest way to understand the insurer's challenge with regard to investing for indexed products is to visualize a dollar of premium coming into such a contract. With this dollar of premium, the insurer must accomplish three basic objectives:

1. provide for the underlying guaranteed return of principal and minimum interest rate;

2. provide for expenses and profit; and

3. provide for the interest credits resulting from index growth.

How an insurer achieves these objectives is based on how it invests the premium deposit. Let's consider each objective separately.

Objective #1: Provide for Guaranteed Principal and Minimum Interest

In order to provide for an EIA's underlying guarantees of preservation of principal and minimum interest rates, insurers typically purchase fixed income instruments

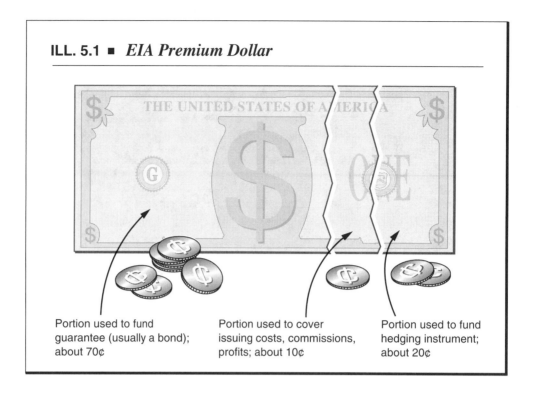

ILL. 5.1 ■ *EIA Premium Dollar*

Portion used to fund guarantee (usually a bond); about 70¢

Portion used to cover issuing costs, commissions, profits; about 10¢

Portion used to fund hedging instrument; about 20¢

such as bonds or zero-coupon bonds. (A zero-coupon bond does not make annual or semi-annual interest payments; instead, all the interest is paid at the bond's maturity.) Using a seven-year point-to-point product as an example, the insurer guarantees that the contract owner will receive a minimum of 110.7 percent of the original premium deposit at the end of seven years. (This 110.7 percent reflects 90 percent of the premium growing at 3 percent per year, the minimum growth that the contract guarantees.) The minimum guarantee on a $100,000 deposit, for instance, would provide for a value of $110,700 at the end of the term. The question then becomes: How much of the premium dollar must be invested in a bond to provide 110.7 percent in seven years? The answer (based on today's interest rate environment) is about 70 percent. In other words, in today's economic climate, an insurer could purchase an investment grade bond for about $70 that would yield approximately $110.70 at a seven-year maturity.

The application of a zero-coupon bond was used in this example because, conceptually, it is easy to understand. However, it is important to note that insurers are generally not purchasing zero-coupon bonds for this purpose because, for most EIA products, there will be a need for liquidity before the end of the contract's term. They are more apt to purchase coupon bonds or mortgage instruments in order to provide for early liquidity if circumstances require it. The death of the contract owner is one such example.

Objective #2: Provide for Expenses and Profit

The second challenge facing the insurer is covering the costs of issuing the contract, including commissions, and providing for a profit. These costs must be absorbed by the premium dollar, thus requiring the insurer to price its products accordingly while remaining competitive in the marketplace.

By far, the largest cost in this category is commissions. Currently, gross compensation on equity indexed annuities runs from about 5 percent to as much as 12 percent of initial premium, which is fairly consistent with other fixed annuities. (There may be a tendency to pay slightly higher commissions on EIAs due to agent and consumer learning curves.)

The second most costly factor in this category is insurer profit. Most carriers price for profit on their indexed annuities in a manner consistent with their other fixed annuities. This translates into 3 percent to 4 percent of initial premium.

The third factor in this category is the cost of issuing the contract. These administrative costs are relatively small and are usually calculated on a per-policy basis.

On average, the total sum of commissions, profits and issuing costs is approximately 10 percent of the premium deposit.

Objective #3: Provide for Indexed Interest Crediting

Funding the guaranteed values and covering the costs of issuing the contract account for approximately 80 percent of the EIA premium dollar the insurer receives, which leaves about 20 percent to fund the remaining challenge—providing for the indexed interest. Many think that the carrier simply invests in the index itself to provide the necessary interest. However, a little bit of analysis shows that this approach will not work. If an insurer were simply to invest 20 percent of an EIA premium dollar in the index, it would realize index growth on only 20 percent of the premium dollar. The contract holder expects an indexed return on 100 percent of his or her premium deposit—after all, that's what the contract offers. This leaves the insurer with having to *leverage* to achieve this return. The most common method of leveraging a stock market investment is through the use of an *option*.

Options

Basically, an option is a securities contract that allows an investor to buy or sell a designated amount of a particular investment—stocks, bonds, futures contracts, etc.—at a specified price within a specified time. A *call option* gives the holder the right to *buy* as described; a *put option* gives the holder the right to *sell*. By purchasing a call option, an investor can participate in a rising market and "lock in" a specified purchase price for the specified investment. By purchasing a put option, an investor could participate in a declining market and lock in a specified sell price. Options are often used by investors to hedge their portfolios against changes in market values. A couple of examples will help clarify this.

Let's assume that Al wants to add 100 shares of IBM to his stock portfolio in a few months. He anticipates the market price of the stock, which has been rising, will continue to increase. Right now he has almost enough money to make the purchase, but he's concerned that the price will rise above the amount he can afford. Al purchases a call option for $900 on the stock of IBM. The call option gives him the right to purchase the stock at a set price (known as the *strike price*)—say, $95 per share—during a specified time period—let's say three months from the date he purchased the option. If Al does not use the call during those three months, it will expire. However, even if Al lets the call expire, all he will lose is the cost of the option ($900), which is a fraction of the cost of the stock.

Al has watched the IBM price per share have a good run. Yesterday he used his call option to purchase the stock at a price of $95 per share, even though its market price is currently $115. Now he is the owner of 100 shares of IBM. He can immediately sell the stock at a gain, as shown below, or he can hold it.

Al Buys		*Al Sells*	
Purchase price per share	$95	Price per share when sold	$115
Shares purchased	100	Shares sold	100
Cost of shares purchased	$9,500	Value of shares sold	$11,500
Cost of option	$900	Cost of investment	$10,400
Total investment	$10,400	Gain	$1,100

Now let's say that Al is concerned that the price of his Boeing stock will decrease over the next nine months. He owns 1,000 shares and they are currently worth $52 per share. To hedge his portfolio against this possible decrease in value, Al could purchase a put option that will give him the right to sell the Boeing stock at, say, $50 a share over the next three months. This option would prove valuable if Al's concern about the decrease in the value of his stock becomes a reality.

Options and Stock Indexes

Almost any item of fluctuating value can be the underlying instrument of an option. Consequently, options can be purchased on indexes, including the S&P 500. The objective when purchasing an index option is obviously not to acquire the right to buy or sell the underlying index but to profit on the direction, degree and timing of the change in the index values or to hedge against losses that market movement can cause in stock positions.

Because index option writers cannot actually deliver an index to satisfy their obligations to option buyers, they deliver cash. A call on an index gives its owner the right to receive, in cash, the option's *intrinsic value*. This is the amount by which the call's strike price is below the index's market value on the day of the call's expiration. For example, let's say an investor purchased a May 1000 call on the S&P 500. On the call's expiration date, the closing value of the index was 1105. Since indexes normally use a multiplier of 100 to convert the strike price into dollar values, the writer of this option would owe the investor $10,500 (the difference between the index value, 1105, and the call's strike price, 1000, multiplied by 100). A put on an index gives its owner the right to receive, in cash, the put's intrinsic value, which would be the amount by which the put's strike price is above the index's closing value on the day of exercise.

Using Index Options for EIAs

For their EIA products, insurers purchase index call options as a hedge to reduce the impact of upward movement in the direction of the index. If the market rises, the calls can be exercised; the insurer receives the cash equivalent of the calls' intrinsic values. If the market does not rise, the options can expire, worthless, at the end of the term. This is really a perfect fit for an EIA contract. The insurer needs to pass along the index increase (or some portion) if the index rises, but owes nothing if the index falls. (Actually, the insurer owes the guaranteed minimum return the contract promises, but this is covered by the fixed income portion of the invested dollar.) Therefore, the insurer uses the remaining 20 percent of the premium dollar to buy call options on the index. Through this strategy, the insurer can control the "cost" it will incur when the index rises and higher rates of return must be credited to its EIA contracts.

EIA call options are typically customized and sold by an investment bank, known as a *counterparty*. The due diligence for the practitioner in this regard requires investigating the safety ratings (credit risk) of the investment bank selling the options. Some very large insurers do not work with an investment bank, but instead will institute a strategy using options available on the major stock exchanges.

The division of a premium dollar into the segments described above—80 percent to cover the contract's guarantees, expenses and profits and 20 percent to hedge the index values—is approximate and can vary significantly from product to product and from insurer to insurer. However, in all cases, the amount of money remaining after funding for the minimum guarantee and the expense/profit portion of the contract will determine the participation rate. The more money available, the higher the participation rate; the less money available, the lower the participation rate. Let's look at this in more detail.

■ WHAT DETERMINES THE PARTICIPATION RATE?

As noted earlier, many EIA contracts (though not all) guarantee their participation rates for the full initial term. When that is the case, determination of the participation rate is only relevant for new money going into new contracts or at contract renewals. (Renewal, of course, occurs at the end of the initial term during the window.) For products that do not guarantee participation rates for the entire initial term, determination of the participation rate will take on an annual significance.

Recall the three basic objectives an insurer must accomplish when investing for equity indexed products:

1. provide for the underlying guaranteed return of principal and minimum interest rate;

2. provide for issuing costs, commission and profit; and

3. provide for the interest credit resulting from index growth.

Meeting each of these challenges involves issues that affect the participation rate. Providing for the contract's underlying guaranteed safety of principal and minimum interest rate involves purchasing a bond. If the bond price increases, there will be less of the premium dollar left to purchase the call options. If there is less money to purchase call options, the insurer's exposure to increasing index values is greater. If the insurer's exposure to index values is greater, the participation rate will be lower.

An EIA's participation rate is entirely dependent on how much of the premium dollar is available to purchase call options and the cost of those call options. In this way, it is a zero-sum process. The insurer has only the premium deposited by the buyer with which to work. Whatever is spent on items other than the options cannot be spent on the options.

With this in mind, it is easy to understand how any expenses or costs the insurer must cover or dollars it must divert will affect participation rates. Those costs include:

- paying commissions

- generating profits

- covering contract issue costs

- purchasing bonds

- purchasing call options

The item having the greatest impact on the participation rate is the item that consumes the greatest portion of the premium dollar—the cost of purchasing bonds. As we know, bond prices are affected by interest rates. As interest rates fall, bond prices rise. As bond prices rise, participation rates fall. As interest rates rise, bond prices fall. As bond prices fall, participation rates rise.

The item having the next greatest impact on participation rates is the cost of the option. Index option costs are a function of various macroeconomic factors and an in-depth discussion is beyond the scope of this text; however, the point can be made in relatively simple terms. Broadly, the price of call options is based on the *implied volatility* of the market: the greater the implied volatility, the higher the cost of the option. Implied volatility can best be described as what buyers and sellers think the market will do in the future. Occasionally this correlates well with the way the market is currently behaving, but often it does not. In fact, just the opposite sometimes occurs. The bottom line is, if implied volatility rises, then the cost of options rises. If the cost of options rises, then (all other factors being equal) the participation rate falls.

Issuing costs, profits and commissions all operate in the same way. Specifically, as the cost of these items rises, the amount left to purchase call options falls. If the amount left to purchase options falls, then the participation rate will also fall.

Example

Keep in mind that rarely is it a clear-cut case of one item rising or falling while all others remain the same. Let's look at an example.

Assume an insurer currently provides for an 85 percent participation rate on its equity indexed annuity product. Since this rate was first set, interest rates have risen by 20 basis points and implied volatility has risen, causing a 10 percent increase in the cost of the call option. The 20 basis point rise in interest rates has caused a 2 percent decrease in the cost of the bonds that the insurer uses to fund the contract's

ILL. 5.2 ■ *Cause and Effect*

If interest rates rise, then . . .	If interest rates fall, then . . .
• *Bond prices fall* • *Participation rates rise* • *Margins fall*	• *Bond prices rise* • *Participation rates fall* • *Margins rise*
If implied volatility rises, then . . .	**If implied volatility falls, then . . .**
• *Options costs rise* • *Participation rates fall* • *Margins rise*	• *Options costs fall* • *Participation rates rise* • *Margins fall*

underlying guarantees. In addition to these two factors, the insurer also had to increase commissions by one percentage point in response to a competitor's introduction of a higher-commissioned product, which was taking away market share. Here are the hypothetical results of these events:

- The interest rate increase yields a 4 percent increase in the participation rate.

- The volatility increase yields a 5 percent decrease in the participation rate.

- The commission increase yields a 7 percent decrease in the participation rate.

- All together, the participation rate decreases by 8 percent.

The 8 percent change in the participation rate will apply to new money purchases only. It will not affect previous deposits, unless the product does not guarantee the initial participation rate for the entire initial term.

Margin Products

As mentioned previously, margin products operate a little differently than participation rate products. Whereas the participation rate is multiplied by the indexed return with the result credited to the contract, the margin is subtracted from the indexed return and the difference is the amount credited to the contract. Therefore, a margin will move in the opposite direction of a participation rate. If participation rates move down, margins will move up. If participation rates move up, margins will move down. Using the example above, here's how a margin product might have behaved:

- The interest rate increase yields a .3 percent decrease in the margin.

- The volatility increase yields a .4 percent increase in the margin.

- The commission increase yields a .6 percent increase in the margin.

- All together, the margin increases by .7 percent.

As is the case with participation products, a change in the margin will apply only to new money, unless the product does not guarantee the margin for the initial term.

■ COUNTERPARTIES

Counterparties, as noted earlier, are outside organizations that provide the call option hedging strategy. A counterparty may be an investment bank, a money management firm or a reinsurance firm. These organizations develop the actual hedging strategy and execute it. Additionally, they guarantee the adequacy of such a strategy in providing the insurer with sufficient funds in the event of growth in the index. If the counterparty fails, then the insurer has the ultimate responsibility to make good for the annuity contract holder. However, it should be noted that once an insurer has written large amounts of EIAs (i.e., hundreds of millions or billions), its solvency may become increasingly tied to the solvency of the counterparty. This is why it is important for a producer to verify the credit rating and financial strength of the insurer issuing the EIA and the counterparty backing it.

■ RESERVES AND SURPLUS

States in which insurers do business require the filing of annual statements that include, along with other information, the insurer's reserve calculations. To ensure that an insurer's reserves will be sufficient to pay future benefits and claims, minimum reserve requirements must be met. Insurers are generally free to hold higher reserves than the minimum.

To calculate minimum reserves for EIAs, actuaries must select one of three permitted methods. Each of the methods is complicated and represents a set of instructions to calculate the reserves. In the simplest of terms, these methods use growth rates for the underlying index in estimating the value of future benefit payments as of the date of the annual statement. In addition to these calculations, actuaries are also required to test the reserves by simulating future cash flows from assets, benefit payments and expenses under a variety of scenarios. If it is found that the assets produce insufficient cash flows, higher reserves may be needed.

Although the rules for minimum reserves provide considerable guidance for the actuary, calculating reserves for EIAs is not an exact science. This is due to a number of things, including being able to choose from the three minimum reserve calculation methods, estimates inherent in the market values of underlying options and assumptions used in cash flow testing, which are usually left to the actuary's best judgment.

Additional reserves are typically calculated for those insurers that prepare annual reports to their corporate shareholders. These are referred to as "GAAP reserves," because they are calculated according to Generally Accepted Accounting Principles (GAAP). In most cases, GAAP reserves for any EIA are equal to its current indexed value.

As with all other annuity products, EIAs affect an insurer's risk-based capital (RBC) requirements. Risk-based capital is a method of measuring an insurer's capital needs and adequacy. However, current formulas used to calculate RBC make no special provisions for EIAs since these formulas were developed long before EIAs became popular. It is possible that the RBC formulas will eventually be changed to account for the unique nature of equity indexed annuities. Until changes are made, however, the RBC formulas that were originally designed for declared-rate fixed annuities will continue to apply.

Adequate surplus is the primary indicator that an insurer's financial condition is healthy. Therefore, an insurer must closely monitor how its surplus is being used. Surplus usage varies by product and is affected by RBC requirements and by the costs the insurer incurs in writing new business. Most insurance products, including annuities, use more surplus than they contribute to surplus in the year that the business is written. Thereafter, insurance products typically make positive contributions to surplus. For EIAs, the amount of surplus used in writing new business is similar to that for declared-rate fixed annuities. This amount tends to be more than that used by variable products and market-value adjusted annuities, and less than that used by most life and health insurance products.

■ SUMMARY

Though a complete and thorough discussion of insurers' EIA investment strategies is well beyond the scope of this text, it is important to know the fundamentals. A basic knowledge will help producers select the right insurer and enable him or her to better explain the workings of EIA products to clients. The next chapter looks at administrative issues that apply to EIAs.

■ CHAPTER REVIEW QUESTIONS

1. When investing an EIA premium dollar, the insurer must consider providing for

   A. profit

   B. issue costs

   C. both A and B

   D. neither A nor B

2. What type of investment do insurers typically utilize to cover the minimum guarantees their EIA contracts provide?

   A. Bonds

   B. Blue-chip stocks

   C. Options

   D. Mutual funds

3. From the insurer's perspective when investing for an EIA product, which of the following requires the largest outlay?

    A. Covering the contract's indexed interest credits

    B. Paying commissions to sales agents

    C. Providing for a profit margin

    D. Covering the contract's minimum guarantees

4. All other factors remaining equal, when interest rates rise

    A. bond prices fall

    B. EIA margins fall

    C. EIA participation rates rise

    D. all of the above occur

5. All other factors remaining equal, when implied volatility rises

    A. EIA margins rise

    B. EIA participation rates rise

    C. put options expire

    D. none of the above occur

6. All EIA insurers use call option strategies packaged by investment banks.

    True or False

7. Under what circumstance(s) would the participation rate on an insurer's new EIA issues decrease?

    A. When market interest rates rise

    B. When the market's implied volatility increases

    C. When bond prices fall

    D. When any of the above occur

6

EIA Administrative Issues

T he previous chapter focused on a number of popular EIA product designs and the investment strategies insurers must employ to support these unique contracts. As we learned, the cost of options to cover an EIA's index-linked interest rate directly affects the contract's participation rate. But the participation rate is only one unique feature of these products; there are many other design options that insurers may incorporate into their EIA contracts. This variety has resulted in a proliferation of product designs. This chapter explores this issue and addresses why there are so many different types of equity indexed annuities. We will also take a brief look at the manner in which these annuity contracts are issued and administratively supported by the insurance company.

■ ■ ■ ■ ■

■ WHY SO MANY EIA DESIGNS?

With few exceptions, practitioners who sell EIAs—and those who are assessing their potential as an addition to their portfolio of products and services—find it increasingly difficult to keep track of the proliferation of EIA designs over the past few years. Different indexing methodologies, varying participation rates, caps, vesting schedules, floors, compound interest, simple interest—all of these things can and do assume different shapes and forms, depending on the specific EIA contract. The prevailing view seems to be that other types of annuities on the market today—fixed rate and variable—are all fairly similar when compared to their counterparts. Why isn't this the case with EIAs?

With standard declared-rate fixed annuities, the major product differences are fairly straightforward: bonus rate vs. no bonus rate; length of surrender charge period; interest rate; liquidity; and commissions. With variable annuities, the most significant product distinctions center around subaccount options and the mechanics of the death benefit. EIAs, by contrast, differ not only in fundamental design (point-to-point, high water mark, annual reset, etc.) but they can entail secondary features such as averaging, caps and vesting, which seem to make the number of product variations increase exponentially. Is it that insurance carriers are striving for product differentiation? Certainly, insurers take product differentiation into account when designing their EIAs, just as they do when designing other types of annuities; however, the explanation goes deeper than this.

The investments that insurers buy to back an EIA product line are available in many more "flavors" than the traditional bonds and mortgages that are used to back non-indexed fixed annuities. In other words, an insurer issuing a standard declared-rate fixed annuity will encounter the same universe of long- and short-term bond rates that its competitors encounter. These bonds and mortgages are rarely customized to suit a particular insurer and their cost does not vary much from carrier to carrier. Consequently, if each insurer must spend the same portion of each premium dollar to buy the bonds that back the annuity contract's interest rate guarantee, there will be a similar amount left over to "subsidize" other product features. The end result is fairly standard and fairly similar product designs among insurers issuing non-indexed fixed annuities.

EIAs are backed not only with bonds (to provide the minimum interest rate guarantees) but with customized option contracts (to provide the index-linked interest). These option contracts are very flexible. They can be structured in any number of ways to suit the financial needs of each carrier and to support a particular product design. This creates the opportunity for much more flexibility in EIA product design. In addition, other factors come into play, such as the amount of the risk the insurer wants to assume, the cost of the options it purchases to back the contract, the insurer's pricing assumptions, the level of field education and support that will be required and the insurer's administrative support systems. Let's briefly examine each of these factors.

The Amount of Risk the Insurer Wants to Assume

Insurance companies assume some unique risks when they issue equity indexed annuities. How they choose to handle this risk will, to a large extent, determine product features and designs. Specifically, these risks are:

1. **The investments purchased to back the EIA will not cover the index-linked interest outlined in the contract in addition to providing the minimum interest rate guarantees.** Some companies face the risk of guaranteeing a contract's participation rates for future years while the supporting investments are purchased on an annual basis. The participation rate guarantee may require a trade-off, such as a cap.

2. **Surrender and withdrawal activity is significantly higher or lower than anticipated.** The risk associated with higher-than-expected surrenders or withdrawals is that the insurer could be forced to liquidate investments at a price that is less than the amount the surrender and withdrawal activity requires. Low surrenders and withdrawals can also be a problem. For example, if the insurer anticipates that 10 percent of its new EIA issues will not persist long enough to receive index-linked returns, it may purchase options to cover 90 percent of its new issues. But if only 5 percent of the new issues terminate prematurely, there will not be "enough" options to go around. Generally speaking, most insurers purchase fixed-income investments to cover their anticipated terminations. Interest earned from these investments may not be sufficient to cover indexed-linked interest for the 5 percent of

new issue holders who did not terminate as expected, especially in a strong bull market.

3. **Mortality deviates significantly from the insurer's assumption.** Mortality risk is the risk that death claims may be higher or lower than anticipated. This is a risk that insurers face with every type of annuity they issue, and mortality risk on EIAs poses no different challenge.

Given the above, insurers will adjust the various features of their EIA contracts to reflect the degree of investment, surrender, withdrawal and mortality risk they are willing to assume.

The Cost of the Insurer's Hedging Strategies

An EIA's design also affects the cost of the options an insurer purchases to back the product's index-linked interest feature. Generally speaking, the more generous the contract's features or the fewer trade-offs a contract entails, the more costly will be the hedging instruments to the insurer. The cost of the options also depends on the current interest rate environment and the implied volatility of the stock market. As these conditions vary, so will the cost of the options. Therefore, insurers must make some assumptions with regard to the cost of their hedging strategies in different types of financial environments. They want to adopt a product design that will be competitive no matter what happens to current market interest rates or the stock market.

The Insurer's Pricing Assumptions

When issuing any type of fixed annuity contract, indexed or not, the insurer must be concerned with the cost of supporting the product, not only from an investment standpoint but administratively as well. This includes systems and marketing support and agent compensation. When all of this support is provided for, the EIA must still meet the insurance company's profit goals and objectives. Some EIA features cost the insurer more than others. This, too, leads to differences in product design.

The Level of Field Education and Support

Successful insurance companies are aware of the experience and expertise of their sales force, another factor that contributes to the choice of one EIA product design versus another. An insurance company that distributes through a large, geographically diverse group of agents without much annuity experience, for example, may choose a very simple point-to-point design with few bells and whistles. The insurer may want to minimize the time necessary to train its sales force so it chooses a design that can be easily explained. On the other hand, an insurer that distributes through stockbrokers may decide to offer a design with more of the bells and whistles to which its sales force may be accustomed.

Administrative Support

An EIA design that cannot be handled effectively and efficiently by the insurer's computer systems and support staff is unlikely to be adopted by that insurer. By modifying the system and procedures, almost any product design can be supported.

ILL. 6.1 ■ *Equity Indexed Annuities on the Market Today*

Indexing Methodology
- Annual reset   51%
- Point-to-point   33%
- High water mark   15%
- Other   1%

Type of Premium
- Single Premium   68%
- Flexible Premium   32%

Features *(% of use in current product designs)*
- Participation rate only   64%
- Margin only   7%
- Margin and participation rate   3%
- Participation rate and cap   24%
- Margin, cap and participation rate   3%
- Features (above) that may change during term   33%
- Averaging   57%
- Vesting schedules   21%
- Explicit surrender charge   85%
- Implicit surrender charge   15%

Interest
- Compound   85%
- Simple   9%
- NA   5%

Free Withdrawal Provisions *(% of use in current product designs)*
- Percent of index value   53%
- Percent of premium   15%
- Percent of guaranteed minimum account value   5%
- Other   13%
- None   13%

Contract Issue Procedures
- Daily   27%
- Weekly   65%
- Bi-monthly   4%
- 4 times per month   3%
- Monthly   1%

Waiver of Surrender Charges
- Nursing home confinement   61%
- Terminal illness   32%
- None   29%
- AD&D   7%
- Unemployment   5%

Source: NFC Consulting Group. Figures are as of 1/99 and are rounded.

However, the insurer needs to carefully weigh the time and expense involved against the desirability of a given design.

As the above makes clear, the decision as to the type of EIA product an insurer brings to the market is influenced by many factors. Knowledge of these factors—and their influence on product designs and options—will help practitioners better understand the product or products they represent.

■ EIA CONTRACT ISSUANCE

Just as there are significant differences between the design and operation of equity indexed annuity contracts compared to declared-rate annuity contracts, so too are there distinctions in the way these contracts are issued and administered.

The process of issuing a fixed annuity contract generally begins when an application and premium payment are received by the insurance company. The application is checked for completeness and to ensure that all company policies and procedures are followed. The premium payment is deposited by the insurer and becomes part of the company's general account assets. Though practices may vary slightly from carrier to carrier, an annuity contract usually becomes effective the day the premium is deposited or within one or two days of its receipt by the insurer. The date a declared-rate annuity contract becomes effective is the date that the premium payment begins earning interest.

The procedures involved with issuing equity indexed annuities are somewhat different. To understand why, we need to return to the concept of how insurers invest EIA dollars to support these contracts. As we know, an insurance company buys bonds or other fixed income investments to support the minimum interest rate guarantees of the EIA. If this were the only procedure involved, the entire process of issuing an EIA would be exactly the same as that involved with declared-rate fixed annuities. However, the insurance company must also purchase other kinds of investments—options—to provide the interest link to the index. These options are usually purchased from a financial counterparty and, from a financial standpoint, it is usually not practical to purchase small numbers of options every day; the financial counterparty generally requires a minimum amount of funds to be invested before it will furnish a customized option contract.

The end result is that some insurance companies may wait until sufficient amounts of premium payments are received before issuing EIA contracts. These "holding" periods can last anywhere from a few days to a week or more. For example, an insurance company might declare that it will issue EIAs once a week on Monday for all premium payments that were received by the previous Thursday. Procedures vary by carrier with respect to the amount of interest (if any) credited during the time between receipt of a premium payment and when the EIA contract is actually issued. The practitioner should be familiar with the procedures of the company with which he or she is doing business.

Keep in mind that not all carriers have such "holding" period delays between the time they receive premium payments and when they issue contracts. Some companies issue contracts on the day they deposit funds into their general accounts.

Annual Statements

For fixed annuity contract owners, state insurance department regulations mandate that insurance companies provide policy statements at least once a year. Among other things, these statements indicate the value of the contract, the interest earned on that value from the prior year, the rate of interest that will be credited to the contract for the coming year and the amount that is available for surrender. Providing this kind of information presents some unique challenges to EIA issuers.

As explained in previous chapters, some types of EIA designs do not credit full interest until the end of the contract term. This is the case with the point-to-point design, for example. Therefore, the only value that can be reported on an annual basis is that created by the minimum interest rate guarantee, which again, is generally 3 percent on 90 percent of the initial premium. Insurance carriers that offer these types of EIA designs have come up with a number of solutions. Some indicate the value of the S&P 500 Index as of each contract anniversary so that the contract owner has an idea of the direction of the index. Other companies may show the surrender value of the contract on each anniversary date. In all cases, however, the insurer shows the contract's guaranteed minimum value on each annual statement. Illustrations 6.2 and 6.3 show examples of two annual statements: one for an annual reset EIA and one for a five-year high water mark EIA.

End of Term Options

Recall that the term of an index annuity is the period of time over which changes in the index are calculated and subsequently credited to the contract. It is, essentially, the measure of the contract's duration. At the end of the term, there is a 30- to 45-day window period, during which the contract owner can decide what he or she wants to do with the contract values. There are four options:

1. The contract owner can renew the contract for a similar term. Some carriers may also allow the contract owner to choose a different length term. If there are explicit surrender charges on the annuity contract, they are usually reinstated for the new term.

2. The contract owner can withdraw his or her money without surrender charges. (Note, however, that federal income taxes and will apply to the earnings and, if the owner is not yet age 59½, a 10 percent penalty may also be imposed. See Ill. 6.4.)

3. The contract may credit nonindex-linked interest on an annual basis thereafter. In other words, it begins to operate like a declared-rate fixed annuity contract wherein the insurance company declares what the current interest rate will be for the coming year. In some cases, contract owners are given the choice of transferring their funds into any other type of fixed annuity contract offered by the insurance company.

4. The contract owner can annuitize the contract, converting its funds into a term certain or lifetime income stream.

Some insurance companies notify the client of his or her choices before the window period begins; others do not. Companies that do not provide notification will instead

ILL. 6.2 ■ *Example of Annual Statement (Annual Reset)*

Altruistic National Life
COMPANY

Statement of Contract Values
Equity Indexed Annuity
Statement Date: 2/15/97

Contract Owner: Charles M. Reilly
Annuitant: Charles M. Reilly
Tax Qualification: Nonqualified
Issue Date: 2/15/96
Premium Deposit: $60,000

Contract Values:

Accumulated Value as of 2/15/96:	$60,000.00
Interest Earned: 14%	$8,400.00
Accumulated Value as of 2/15/97:	$68,400.00
Surrender Value:	$63,579.74

Index Data:

S&P 500 Levels
As of 2/15/96:	648.08
As of 2/15/97:	788.39
Increase from 2/15/96 to 2/15/97:	21.65%

Contract Rates:

Index Participation Rate:	85.00%
Cap:	14.00%
Floor:	0.00%

The Index participation rate for the next contract year will be 85.00% (used for calculations on 2/15/98), the Index floor will be 0.00% and the Index cap will be 14.00%.

ILL. 6.3 ▪ *Example of Annual Statement (High Water Mark)*

Altruistic National Life
COMPANY

Annual Statement of Contract Values
Equity Indexed Annuity
Statement Date: 1/1/97

Contract Owner:	Louise McGlaughlin	Term:	01/01/96 – 01/01/01
Annuitant:	Louise McGlaughlin	Term Length:	5 years
Initial Premium:	$100,000	S&P Starting Value:	615
Issue Date:	January 1, 1996	Participation Rate:	85%

Current Vested Indexed Value Calculation (20% Vested)

S&P 500 starting value:	615
S&P 500 value on 1/1/97:	788
Indexed value as of 1/1/96:	$100,000.00
Credited index increases (20% vested):	$ 4,782.11
Withdrawals:	$ 0.00
Indexed value as of January 1, 1997:	$104,782.11

Surrender Value Calculation

Surrender value as of January 1, 1996:		$90,000.00
Interest credited at 3%:	$2,700.00	
Withdrawals:	$ 0.00	
Surrender value increase:		$ 2,700.00
Surrender value as of January 1, 1997:		$92,700.00

Minimum Value at End of Term (100% Vested)

$109,444.44
Assumes contract is held to end of term, with no further increase in
the S&P 500 Index and no withdrawals.

Your Altruistic Equity Indexed Annuity provides earnings based on the price change in
the S&P 500 Index over a five-year period. Index increases will be credited to your indexed
values each year on a pro rata vesting basis as described in your contract. Index increases are
based on the highest S&P 500 anniversary value during the five-year term. Your contract
values are guaranteed to be at least equal to your initial premium less any withdrawals.

indicate in the annuity contract and in their sales materials what automatically happens at the end of the term if they do not hear otherwise from the contract owner. Therefore, it is important that the practitioner be knowledgeable about the procedures followed by the insurance companies with whom he or she does business.

Annual Reset EIAs

Annual reset EIAs need further clarification. Carriers define the term of their annual reset EIAs as the length of the contract's surrender charge period. For example, an annual reset design with seven years of surrender charges would provide one or more of the choices cited above at the end of the seventh year. Other annual reset designs do not provide the client with any specific choices at the end of the surrender charge period. It is assumed that the contract is fully liquid at that time. The contract owner can either move the funds or continue to receive index-linked interest for as long as the contract is owned.

Disclosure Notices

Most insurance companies require that buyers of annuity contracts acknowledge and sign a disclosure notice at the time of sale. Also known as a "summary of benefits," this short form summarizes some of the important features and benefits of the EIA contract. It might also contain a tabular summary of guaranteed minimum contract values, surrender values and/or examples of how the contract may credit interest when the index rises, falls or remains steady. A copy of the signed disclosure notice usually must be submitted to the insurance company with the application in order for the contract to be issued. Another copy is left with the client and a third copy may be kept by the practitioner. Illustration 6.4 shows an example of one type of EIA disclosure notice.

Illustration of Contract Features and Values

Many fixed annuities today are presented to a potential buyer with an illustration that projects the contract's future values. The one- or two-page illustration typically shows the accumulated values and contract surrender values based on the initial premium payment, the current initial interest rate (usually guaranteed for the first year) and thereafter the guaranteed minimum interest rate of 3 percent or 4 percent.

Creating illustrations for EIAs presents quite a different challenge. Because the interest rate to be credited to the annuity is not known in advance, it cannot be illustrated. The only values that can be accurately illustrated are the guaranteed minimum contract values. Yet because the EIA is so unique, insurance companies and state insurance regulators felt that EIA buyers needed to be provided with an expectation of what their future interest rate(s) might be. Their concern was that some buyers may not understand that in years of poor stock market performance, there might be no index-linked interest credited to the annuity (even though there would be no loss of principal in these cases).

To address this issue, various proposals have been put forth as to how potential values of EIA contracts might be illustrated. At the time of this text's publication, there was not unanimous industry agreement as to how this can best be accomplished. In order to aid their buyers' understanding of the interest crediting mechanics of the

ILL. 6.4 ■ *Example of EIA Disclosure Notice*

**Altruistic National Life
COMPANY**

Summary of Features and Benefits
Equity Indexed Annuity

You have purchased Altruistic National Life's Equity Indexed Annuity. In order to assure that you understand the nature and features of this product and that you understand the terms of the contract, please read the following and then sign and date below.

1. Altruistic's Equity Indexed Annuity is a tax-deferred annuity. Your principal is guaranteed by Altruistic. It is possible that you could lose principal if you withdraw funds from the annuity during the first four years, due to the 7 percent surrender charge.

2. Any growth or build-up within the annuity will not be taxable until such time you withdraw funds from it. Any withdrawal prior to age $59\frac{1}{2}$ is subject to a tax penalty of 10 percent.

3. After the first contract year, you may withdraw, each year and without surrender charge, up to 10 percent of the annuity's accumulated value.

4. During the initial seven-year contract term, your annuity values will grow in accordance with the following:

- The annual rate of return of the S&P 500 Composite Stock Price Index.

- The participation rate, which is the percentage of the gain of the S&P 500 Composite Stock Price Index that will be credited to your contract values. For example, if the S&P Index gains 12 percent during a contract year and your participation rate is 85 percent, your gain would be 10.20 percent (12% x 85%). The current participation rate is indicated on page 2 of your annuity contract and is guaranteed for the first year of the contract. Though it is expected that the participation rate will remain the same throughout the seven-year term of your contract, it is subject to change after the first contract year.

ILL. 6.4 ■ *Example of EIA Disclosure Notice (Cont.)*

**Altruistic National Life
COMPANY**

- The cap. The cap is the maximum percentage that will be credited to your annuity account value each year. The current cap is indicated on page 2 of your contract and is guaranteed for the first year of the contract. Though it is expected that the cap will remain the same throughout the seven-year term of your contract, it is subject to change after the first contract year.

- The floor. The floor is the minimum annual percentage increase that is applied to your contract values. It will never be less than 0 percent, which means that your account value can never decline due to a decrease in the value of the S&P 500 Composite Stock Price Index.

5. At the end of your contract's seven-year term, you may, within 30 days, elect one of the following options:

- Continue with the contract for another seven-year term

- Withdraw your funds

- Exchange on a tax-free basis for another annuity

The performance of the S&P 500 Index is a factor used in the calculation of your annuity's interest rate. The historical performance of the S&P 500 Index should not be considered a representation of how the Index will perform in the future or how much interest you will earn.

_____	_____
Owner	Date
_____	_____
Joint Owner	Date
_____	_____
Agent	Date

Submit to Home Office with Application

"Standard & Poor's," "S&P 500" and "Standard & Poor's 500" are trademarks of The McGraw-Hill Companies, Inc., and have been licensed for use by Altruistic National Life Insurance Company. Altruistic's Equity Indexed Annuity is not sponsored, endorsed, sold or promoted by Standard & Poor's and Standard & Poor's makes no representation regarding the advisability of purchasing this product.

EIA, some insurance companies provide hypothetical examples of a "worst case," "best case" and "average case" interest crediting scenario using actual historical index values. Others explain in narrative fashion how the EIA contract values may increase or decrease depending upon movements in the index and the contract's interest crediting formula. Regardless of the way the explanation is given, most carriers do not provide the client with a personalized illustration. Instead, the explanation is usually contained in the disclosure statement or sales material provided to the client at time of sale.

■ SUMMARY

The proliferation of equity indexed annuity designs available can be traced to many factors: the investment strategies they require, the costs they entail, the amount of risk the issuer wants to assume, the experience of the insurer's field force and the technological capabilities an insurer may—or may not—have are only a few factors that drive the type of product a carrier brings to market. The fact that there are so many choices means that the producer has greater opportunity to match a product with client needs and objectives. At the same time, the variety of products and the myriad of different features they offer means the producer has the responsibility to understand the product he or she represents. In the next chapter, we will discuss how EIAs can be used to address client needs, specifically retirement planning.

■ CHAPTER REVIEW QUESTIONS

1. The date a fixed annuity contract becomes effective is

   A. the date that the application is signed by the applicant

   B. the date that the application is received by the insurer

   C. the date that the premium payment begins earning interest

   D. the first day of the first month after the insurer receives the premium payment

2. Which of the following is shown on all annual statements for EIA contracts?

   A. Full indexed interest to be credited to the contract for its term

   B. The contract's guaranteed minimum value

   C. Both A and B

   D. Neither A nor B

3. Surrender or withdrawal activity that is less than what the insurer anticipated does not pose a risk to the insurer and, therefore, will not affect an EIA's design.

   True or False

4. All of the following are reasons why there are so many different types of EIA product designs, EXCEPT

   A. the variety and flexibility of the bonds and mortgages insurers purchase to back their EIA products

   B. the variety and flexibility of the options contracts insurers purchase to back their EIA products

   C. the level of support and education insurers provide to their field forces

   D. the capabilities of insurers' administrative and computer systems

5. All of the following are common options an EIA contract holder has at the end of his or her term, EXCEPT

   A. renew the contract for a similar term

   B. withdraw the annuity's funds without surrender charges

   C. annuitize the contract's funds

   D. exchange the contract for a life insurance policy

7

Planning with Equity Indexed Annuities

F or many individuals and for many different types of investors, equity indexed annuities can play an important role in helping shape their long-term financial plans. Ideally suited for retirement planning, EIAs offer a number of unique opportunities and benefits. However, as is the case with any financial product or any investment, it's imperative that the producer understand when EIAs are appropriate, where they fit and why. This chapter will explore these issues. In addition, we will take a look at the evolving demographics of the EIA buyer.

■ ■ ■ ■ ■

■ POSITIONING EQUITY INDEXED ANNUITIES

The deferred annuity is a long-term planning product, suitable for long-term investment horizons and long-term accumulation needs. For most, the general objective annuities address is retirement and they are ideally suited for this purpose: funds accumulate on a tax-deferred basis; the many income options available upon annuitization help individuals manage cash flow; and, assuming a life-income payout option is elected, there is the guarantee that the income cannot be outlived. As the ranks of retirees continue to grow and as life expectancies continue to rise, the need for annuities will certainly increase.

Accordingly, this is how the EIA should be positioned. By providing the same tax-deferred build-up of funds, the same guarantee of principal and the same kinds of income options as declared-rate fixed annuities, an EIA offers an excellent way to accumulate and distribute retirement assets. But it also goes a few steps further. By offering interest linked to an equity index, the EIA becomes an attractive alternative for those who would otherwise have to look to riskier investments for a higher investment yield. In this way, the EIA offers additional planning benefits:

- an opportunity to outpace the rate of inflation;

- a potential for higher market returns without corresponding market risk; and

- a unique choice for the conservative portion of an asset allocation program.

ILL. 7.1 ■ *Rates of Return, Selected Periods*

	1927–1997	1967–1997	1977–1997	1987–1997
	(Percent per year, compounded annually)			
Large Company Stocks	11.0%	12.5%	15.4%	16.8%
Small Company Stocks	12.9%	15.3%	18.1%	13.8%
Long-Term Corporate Bonds	5.7%	8.4%	9.9%	9.8%
Long-Term Gov't. Bonds	5.2%	8.0%	9.8%	10.0%
Intermediate-Term Gov't. Bonds	5.3%	8.3%	9.1%	7.8%
U.S. Treasury Bills	3.8%	6.7%	7.2%	5.4%
Rate of Inflation	3.2%	5.3%	5.0%	3.5%

Source: Used with permission. © 1998 Ibbotson Associates, Inc. All rights reserved. (Certain portions of this work were derived from copyrighted works of Roger G. Ibbotson and Rex Sinquefield.)

Let's consider each.

The Potential to Outpace the Rate of Inflation

Without question, one of the benefits of investing in the stock market is the real rate of return it produces. Over extended periods of time, investing in equities has been proven to outpace the rate of inflation and has done so far better than fixed-interest rate investments such as bonds and Treasury bills. As Ill. 7.1 shows, the rates of return on large and small company stocks over select periods are significantly higher than the rates of inflation for those same periods compared to the rates of return on corporate bonds, government bonds and Treasury bills.

The potential to outpace inflation is significant since inflation erodes purchasing power and undermines the effort of saving for retirement. For example, assume Mary directs $100,000 that she has saved for retirement into a certificate of deposit IRA earning 6 percent interest. At the end of one year, she will have earned $6,000 in interest. However, the rate of inflation during the year was 3 percent, so Mary's real rate of return on her money is actually only 3 percent (6.0 percent return −3.0 percent rate of inflation), or $3,000. Alternatively, Mary could invest her $100,000 IRA in stocks, where the opportunity for a far better return exists. Again, historically, equities have outperformed all other types of investments and have more than beat the rate of inflation. But there is a price to pay for these potentially higher earnings: the risk that the investment will result in loss of principal. So what does the investor do? Divert retirement savings into safe but low-yielding investments, sure to be affected by inflation? Or risk the loss of principal for higher returns?

Until the introduction of the equity indexed annuity, investors who did not want to risk principal had little opportunity to offset the effects of inflation on their retirement savings. In fact, due to their fear of loss, many conservative savers have avoided the market completely, choosing instead to utilize guaranteed products. With an EIA, they do not have to choose one option over another; the product will allow them, at once, to market-link their interest earnings, which are likely to be higher than those offered by other safe products, *and* rest assured that there will be no loss of principal. Though no one can predict how the equity markets will perform in the future and history is no guarantee of future performance, equity-linked investments such as EIAs offer the potential to achieve a rate of return higher than the rate of inflation.

Risk vs. Return

To fully appreciate the value of the equity indexed annuity, it is important to understand the relationship between risk and return and to be able to weigh the balance between the client's tolerance for the former and his or her desire for the latter.

Earlier in the text, we discussed the concept of risk as it relates to the insurance industry in general and to the annuity product specifically. Fixed annuities provide investors with a guarantee against loss of principal. The trade-off is that the return on a fixed annuity (or on any financial product that guarantees the return of principal) is usually lower than the return that might be achieved on a financial product that does not guarantee return of principal. The concept is often illustrated with a pyramid, such as that shown in Ill. 7.2. Investments that pose little or no risk to principal form the base of the financial pyramid.

As one moves up the pyramid, the potential for greater returns increases, but so does the risk of loss of principal. The unique opportunity the equity indexed annuity presents is the potential for returns that are greater than those available with money-

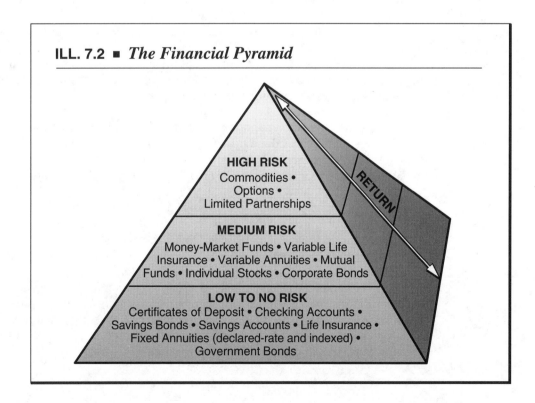

ILL. 7.2 ■ *The Financial Pyramid*

HIGH RISK
Commodities •
Options •
Limited Partnerships

MEDIUM RISK
Money-Market Funds • Variable Life
Insurance • Variable Annuities • Mutual
Funds • Individual Stocks • Corporate Bonds

LOW TO NO RISK
Certificates of Deposit • Checking Accounts •
Savings Bonds • Savings Accounts • Life Insurance •
Fixed Annuities (declared-rate and indexed) •
Government Bonds

RETURN

ILL. 7.3 ■ *Modern Portfolio Theory*

In 1959, Professor Harry Markowitz developed what many consider to be the model that underlies modern portfolio theory. Prior to Markowitz, the concepts of risk and return were only vaguely recognized. Investors knew that they should not put all of their eggs in a single basket, but it was Markowitz who developed a quantitative approach to diversification. He made the assumption that the average investor is a cautious individual who wants to assume only a minimum of risk in attempting to achieve the greatest possible return. This led to the concept of the *efficient portfolio*, which can be defined in terms of either risk or return: it is one that offers the greatest expected return for a given level of risk or one that offers the smallest risk for a given level of expected return. Thus, modern portfolio theory and the efficient portfolio allow an investor to define a level of risk he or she is willing to assume—aggressive to conservative—and maximize the expected return for this level. Alternatively, an investor could target an expected level of portfolio return and minimize the risk at this level. Markowitz recognized that since risk and return are the two most significant factors to an investor, they should be the defining criteria—and that which should be optimized—when constructing a portfolio.

---

market funds, savings accounts, CDs and even fixed rate annuities, but with no additional risk.

A look at the financial pyramid might lead one to believe that risk-averse investors are more apt to invest in the products and investments that form the base of the pyramid while those who are more risk tolerant will invest in products that are positioned nearer the top. This may or may not be true. Even risk-tolerant investors will earmark some portion of their investment dollars for "safe money" investments. The practitioner should not overlook this fact. Where funds are invested is a good indication of how the client feels about them. Funds invested in money markets, passbook savings accounts or CDs, for instance, are certainly examples of investments where guarantee of principal is important.

Risk-averse clients, on the other hand, *may* have trouble investing in the vehicles that are situated toward the top of the financial pyramid. Though they might acknowledge that they should be investing a portion of their savings more aggressively to counteract inflation, they may have trouble actually doing so. In 1994, the Investment Company Institute, which is the trade organization for the mutual fund industry, conducted a survey regarding shareholders' attitudes about risk. Of those surveyed, the ICI found that 27 percent of mutual fund investors were fairly cautious about taking risk and believed that it is best to "play it safe" and avoid all investments they regard as risky. This group was the least likely to own stock mutual funds. The ICI survey highlights the potential danger of a practitioner categorically characterizing someone as a "stock market investor" or a "mutual fund investor" without digging any deeper to determine his or her real feelings regarding investable dollars. The survey also supports the notion that the type of vehicle in which a client has invested funds can provide a clue as to his or her risk tolerance for that particular amount of money.

Equity Indexed Annuities and Asset Allocation

Equity indexed annuities can be used to support the strategy of *asset allocation.* Asset allocation simply means dividing, or allocating, an investor's savings into various types of investments that can be expected to perform differently in different types of financial environments. The value of such a strategy is that if market conditions cause one type of investment to perform poorly, another type of investment may perform well. Over the long term, a client's return is enhanced because performance in poor years balances out. Simply put, asset allocation is a means of increasing return while controlling risk in one's investment portfolio. This principle is one of the foundations of *modern portfolio theory* (see Ill. 7.3).

How exactly do annuities fit into an asset allocation strategy? Take a look at the graph. It shows four quadrants of an asset allocation/ risk-return model. Assume that the center point represents a client's current investment position and he has asked you to help him reallocate. Moving that point to Quadrant 4 is the worst thing you could do. This means your client will be taking on more risk with lower returns. Quadrants 2 and 3 may represent improvements in

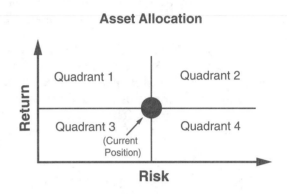

Asset Allocation

the client's portfolio, depending on his or her risk tolerance. A client with a high risk tolerance could move to Quadrant 2 to get a better return and a client with a lower risk tolerance could move to Quadrant 3 and give up some return. In recognition of what happens in Quadrants 2, 3 and 4, now look at Quadrant 1. It's a win-win situation. The client gets higher returns with less risk.

Equity indexed annuities can help move clients into Quadrant 1. But how exactly do EIAs meet the very essence of an asset allocation strategy when one is attempting to increase return without increasing risk? A comparison to other fixed interest financial products may be helpful. Fixed annuities are typically compared to CDs, bonds or bond mutual funds. Each comparison requires its own analysis, but it is fair to say that, in any case, utilizing a fixed annuity (especially an EIA) will either increase return with little change to risk or generate similar returns with less risk. Let's take a brief look at each.

Comparing EIAs to CDs

Comparing the EIA to a certificate of deposit requires some understanding of credit risk. Since CDs are backed by the Federal Deposit Insurance Corporation (FDIC) and the U.S. Treasury, they are safer than annuities. However, a couple of points should be made. First, the FDIC guarantee covers CD balances of $100,000 or less. This puts balances of more than $100,000 at risk. And, in fact, investors have experienced losses on these balances. On the other hand, principal losses on fixed annuities occurred only once. This is obviously the record of a very safe product. Furthermore, annuities almost always carry higher interest rates than CDs and, because their earnings are tax deferred, the marginal earnings advantage is even greater. The result is that for a small increase in risk, a substantial rate advantage can be achieved. This is the essence of asset allocation.

Comparing EIAs to Bonds and Bond Funds

Comparing an equity indexed annuity to a bond or bond fund requires another view of risk. From a credit risk perspective, bonds and bond funds can be as safe as fixed annuities (if high quality bonds are used), but not from a market risk perspective.

As we've discussed, bonds and bond funds fluctuate in value depending on market interest rates. As interest rates rise, bonds and bond funds fall in value and as interest rates fall, bonds and bond funds rise in value. By comparison, fixed annuities (other than market value adjusted designs) have no market risk.

Some would argue that bonds do not have market risk because they can be held to maturity and redeemed for their full value. This is true, but the fact remains that a bond's value will fluctuate until such time. Therefore, if events necessitate a need for funds and an investor must cash in his or her bond prior to maturity, he or she may suffer a loss. And the loss could be huge. In 1994 alone, many bonds (and bond mutual funds) were down 20 percent or more.

From a return standpoint, yields on declared-rate fixed annuities are comparable to an intermediate term bond or bond fund. The yield on an EIA—due to its link to the equity market—may be even higher. Ultimately, the result is that for a similar or higher yield, significant market risk can be eliminated by using fixed indexed annuities. Again, this epitomizes the essence of asset allocation.

As the above examples indicate, an equity indexed annuity can serve as an integral part of an asset allocation program. It enables the owner to achieve equity-linked rates of return while guarding against downward market movement. Even risk-tolerant investors—those who have no trouble investing in mutual funds or variable annuities and who may consider CDs and money-market funds too "stodgy"—might find the EIA a suitable vehicle for the conservative portion of their asset allocation mix.

■ QUALIFIED FUNDS: SPECIAL CONSIDERATIONS

EIAs are designed to provide the buyer with an opportunity for potentially greater growth on his or her funds with protection from market risk. The EIA would therefore seem to be well-suited for IRA money or other types of qualified funds that a consumer may not utilize for many years. For the most part, this is true. However, the practitioner must be aware of the implications that an EIA's contract term may have on required distributions. Generally speaking, distributions from traditional IRAs must begin no later than April 1 following the year the owner turns 70½ and continue every year thereafter. If the term of the EIA contract extends beyond the buyer's required distribution beginning date, he or she may be faced with the choice of having to pay some kind of penalty charge—whether assessed by the insurer for surrendering the contract early or by the IRS for failing to take the required distribution.

In addition, some EIA contracts credit interest only annually or only at the end of the contract's term. If required distributions must be taken before interest is credited, the contract owner could realize less gain or interest than otherwise would have been credited had the funds remained in the contract.

Some insurers have recognized the special circumstances pertaining to qualified funds and required distributions and do allow contract values to be withdrawn without application of surrender charges. Again, it is incumbent upon the practitioner to know how the contracts he or she sells address this issue.

■ COMPARING FINANCIAL PRODUCTS

When discussing EIAs and their role in retirement planning, it is likely that the practitioner will be asked by the client to compare and/or contrast the EIA to other financial products or investment options. A word of caution is in order. Good market conduct requires that the practitioner merely provide a brief explanation of how EIAs differ from these products. The explanation should not position the EIA as a superior alternative to any of these products since they all have their place in a well-rounded retirement portfolio. Furthermore, a direct comparison of a nonregistered EIA product to a registered securities product or any attempt to promote the EIA as a consistently superior alternative can have negative market conduct implications. Presenting a nonregistered product as if it were a security is a violation of securities law.

That said, it is important for the practitioner to have a solid understanding of how EIAs are similar and dissimilar to other alternatives. Illustration 7. 4 compares a number of financial products.

■ IDENTIFYING THE EIA BUYER

When determining the suitability of any type of financial product for a client, the practitioner must know the client's needs. A good rule of thumb when deciding whether an EIA would be appropriate is to determine whether that client would first be a good candidate for *any* fixed annuity. In general, fixed annuity candidates have a relatively long investment horizon and are looking for safety of principal and yield. Buyers of fixed annuities are typically conservative, risk-averse individuals. Tax-deferral, guaranteed income options and cash flow security are also important. Chances are good that if a client would be a potential buyer of a traditional declared-rate fixed annuity, he or she may also be a good candidate for an EIA. However, even though most fixed annuity buyers are conservative individuals, the practitioner should not overlook the fact that the following may also be likely prospects for EIAs:

- **Bond and bond mutual fund investors.** In a quest for good yields and safety of principal, many investors purchase bonds and bond mutual funds. This is typically a good strategy as long as interest rates remain steady or fall. However, as we've learned, when interest rates rise, the value of a bond or a bond mutual fund falls. Over the years, many investors have been unpleasantly surprised by this reality. Their quest for safety then leads them back to vehicles such as money-market funds and CDs which provide safety

ILL. 7.4 ■ *Financial Products Comparison Chart*

	Declared-Rate Fixed Annuity	Equity Indexed Fixed Annuity	Variable Annuity	Equity Indexed Mutual Fund	Stock	Bond
Tax Deferral	Yes	Yes	Yes	No[1]	No[1]	No[1]
Death Benefit	Yes	Yes	Yes	No	No	No
Guarantee of Principal	Yes	Yes[2]	No[3]	No	No	No
Lifetime Income	Yes	Yes	Yes	No	No	No
Earnings Tied to Market Performance	No	Yes	Yes	Yes	Yes	Yes
Minimum Interest Guarantee	Yes	Yes	No[3]	No	No	No
Surrender Charge	Yes	Yes[4]	Yes[5]	Maybe	No	No
Pre-59½ Early Withdrawal Penalty	Yes	Yes	Yes	No[1]	No[1]	No[1]
Management Fees	No	No	Yes	Yes	No	No
Dividends	No	No	Yes	Yes	Yes	No (coupon)

[1] Unless held in a traditional IRA

[2] If held for term

[3] Any funds allocated to the fixed (general assets) account *are* covered by a minimum rate guarantee and principal may be guaranteed.

[4] Some products do not have explicit surrender charges; instead, there may be an implicit loss of some or all indexed interest, depending on the design.

[5] Unless no-load

of principal but little inflation protection. The EIA provides safety of principal as well as the potential to outpace inflation.

- **Clients who are accustomed to risk on a portion of their invested savings.** As mentioned earlier in this chapter, it is a fact that even aggressive investors have some portion of their retirement savings dollars earmarked for safe money investing. In the past 10 years or so, many investors have enjoyed healthy returns from stock market investing. The EIA provides an opportunity for the risk-tolerant stock market investor to "lock in" some of the gains he or she achieved over the years. By putting those funds in an EIA, the gains are secured. Beyond that, the client still has the opportunity to real-ize index-linked interest on the funds without risk to principal.

- **Split annuity owners.** For individuals who have an immediate need for income but desire to preserve principal, the split annuity is often used. With a split annuity, the owner invests his or her premium into two vehicles: an immediate annuity, which generates income, and a deferred annuity, which accumulates funds. Using the EIA for the deferred portion of the split annu-ity provides an opportunity for the owner to achieve a greater return on that segment of the money.

Demographics

The EIA market is relatively new and a demographic profile of the EIA buyer has been evolving since 1994. According to a 1997 Gallup survey, the average age of declared-rate fixed annuity buyers is 65. The average age of an EIA purchaser is 57. The equity indexed annuity seems to be reaching a younger clientele than the indus-try has historically experienced. Indeed, consumer focus group research indicates that even younger buyers—those in the 45 to 55 year age group—show an interest in EIAs. This can be attributed to two reasons. One is that today's younger consum-ers are very aware of their own personal need to save for retirement as the availabil-ity of federally sponsored savings programs and traditional pension plans continues to decline. The other reason is that there are a fair number of young consumers who are risk averse. Though one might assume that younger individuals as a group are more risk tolerant in their investing strategies—that with the many years they have before retiring, they would be willing to withstand some periods of poor market per-formance in return for potentially superior long-term results—this is not necessarily the case. There are a fair number of younger consumers who cannot tolerate loss of principal under any circumstances.

Additional data indicates that slightly more men purchase EIAs than women (52 percent vs. 48 percent). Also, a slightly greater percentage of EIA contracts are issued on a nonqualified basis as compared to those that are established as IRAs or other qualified plans (54 percent vs. 46 percent).

■ SUMMARY

The equity indexed annuity offers a number of unique benefits that can enhance an individual's retirement savings portfolio. By providing tax-deferred accumulation of funds, a guarantee of principal and structured income options *plus* the potential for higher market returns and the corresponding opportunity to outpace inflation, the EIA can be ideal for those who need and want to augment their retirement plans. In this way, an equity indexed annuity adds dimension to an asset allocation pro-gram by providing the opportunity for greater returns with little to no risk. The ideal prospect for an EIA is the individual who would be a candidate for *any* fixed annu-ity: conservative, risk averse and with a long investment horizon. By the same token, even aggressive investors who do not shy away from risk usually earmark a portion of their savings as "safe money." EIAs are ideal for safe money investing, no matter what level of risk an individual wants to assume. However, the fact that EIAs offer these unique opportunities and benefits does not relieve the practitioner of the due diligence responsibility he or she has when marketing these products. The very nature of the product—and the trade-offs it entails—requires a higher level of consumer education, which is the subject of the next chapter.

■ CHAPTER REVIEW QUESTIONS

1. Which of the following statements regarding risk tolerance is true?

   A. Most risk-tolerant investors still earmark a portion of their investment dollars for "safe" investments.

   B. Most risk-averse investors do not invest in financial products that are positioned at the top of the financial pyramid.

   C. Both A and B

   D. Neither A nor B

2. Historically, which of the following types of investments has proven to outpace inflation at the highest rate?

   A. Stocks

   B. Corporate bonds

   C. Government bonds

   D. Fixed annuities

3. How do equity indexed annuities support an asset allocation strategy?

   A. By providing for greater returns with greater risk

   B. By providing for lower returns with lower risk

   C. By providing for greater returns with lower risk

   D. By providing for lower returns with greater risk

4. Which of the following investment objectives does an equity indexed annuity NOT address?

   A. Safety of principal

   B. Short-term investment horizon

   C. Guaranteed rate of return

   D. Asset management

5. All of the following statements regarding EIA buyers are true EXCEPT

   A. They are generally younger than traditional fixed annuity buyers.

   B. They are likely to be men.

   C. They are seeking a qualified plan for their retirement dollars.

   D. They are risk averse.

8

Product Due Diligence

I n the last chapter, we explored the equity indexed annuity's role in retirement planning and the potential it offers for safe money investing. In this chapter, we examine additional issues the practitioner must understand in order to help clients make informed decisions about these products. As we've learned, EIAs come in many flavors, and individual product designs and features can vary quite a bit. It is the practitioner's responsibility to fully understand the nature of the product he or she represents and to be able to explain its features to potential buyers. This includes a frank explanation of the trade-offs associated with the guarantees EIAs provide. We will also take a closer look at some historical EIA interest crediting scenarios for various designs. Certainly, "historical" interest crediting behavior is limited due to the fact that these products are relatively new; however, we will be able to gain a general sense of how different EIA designs will operate in certain market environments. Finally, we'll offer a number of guidelines for selling EIAs, to ensure that the practitioner remains on solid ground when presenting these products.

■ ■ ■ ■ ■

■ THE PRACTITIONER'S RESPONSIBILITIES

Equity indexed annuities have been described as a "win-win" product, a "have-your-cake-and-eat-it-too" financial investment. They have also been criticized for their complexity and the cumulative effect of the limitations that are inherent to many product designs. The fact is, EIAs are not appropriate savings or investment vehicles for everyone, but for many, they will be ideal. For the practitioner who sells EIAs, the task is to determine when and how they will benefit a client and, to do so, a degree of due diligence is required. This means that the practitioner must be able to explain the product thoroughly, accurately and fairly and provide all pertinent information—pro and con—so that the client can make an informed buying decision. This responsibility can be fulfilled if the practitioner follows certain guidelines:

- He or she evaluates the EIA products and understands how they function. This includes analyzing the products' features and becoming familiar with the procedures the insurer follows with respect to contract issuance.

- He or she determines the client's needs and objectives, and fairly assesses whether an equity indexed annuity could help the client meet those needs or achieve those objectives.

- He or she is committed to educating the client about the product, which requires a balanced presentation of its limitations as well as its benefits.

- He or she remains aware of the manner in which the product is sold and what attributes are emphasized.

- He or she understands the EIA's place in a diversified portfolio and how it might support a client's total financial plan in conjunction with other products and other investments. An EIA is not always a substitute for, nor a better choice than, say, an indexed mutual fund or other such investment. It is simply another choice that may be appropriate, given a client's individual situation.

The remainder of this chapter is devoted to explaining how an EIA representative can practice due diligence by focusing on these and other issues.

■ EVALUATING AN EIA CONTRACT

EIA contracts are relatively new and consumers are still learning about them. They are characterized by a number of unique features unfamiliar to the average buyer. Furthermore, how these features operate within the context of the contract—and in conjunction with each other—will determine how the contract credits interest. In the process of analyzing and comparing products, it is not simply a matter of evaluating a contract's provisions and features individually; rather, the practitioner must review all aspects of a specific design and understand how they work in tandem. Only then can a product's benefits and potential be assessed. And only then will the practitioner be able to adequately explain the trade-offs the client must accept in exchange for the contract's guarantees. Let's review what some of these trade-offs may be.

Dividends

Because the interest credited to equity indexed annuities is based on a stock market index, the issue of dividends is frequently raised and just as frequently it is misunderstood—by practitioners and buyers alike. It is worth repeating that equity indexed annuities that are linked to a price index like the S&P 500 are *not* credited with dividends on the stocks that compose the index.* This means that the return credited to an EIA will not be the same as the return one would derive by investing directly in those stocks. Whereas the EIA will reflect the increase in the *price* of the indexed stocks, the value of the stocks themselves would include any dividends that were payable. If one is comparing returns, this will make a difference. For example, assume Joan purchased 10 shares of stock at $10 per share. During the first year she

---

* It should be noted that a very small number of new EIAs have been designed to include dividends in their interest-crediting methodology; however, their participation rates are considerably lower than similarly designed products that do not reflect dividends.

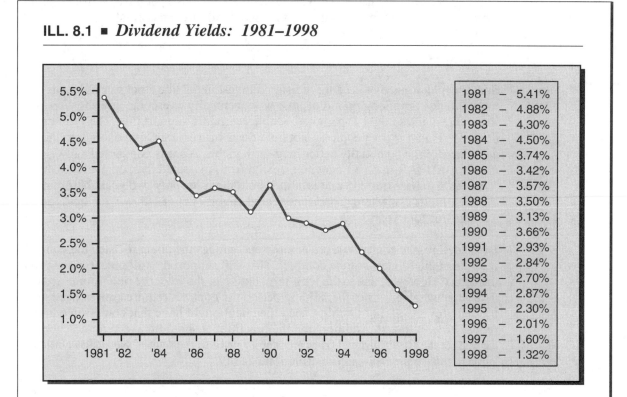

ILL. 8.1 ■ *Dividend Yields: 1981–1998*

1981	–	5.41%
1982	–	4.88%
1983	–	4.30%
1984	–	4.50%
1985	–	3.74%
1986	–	3.42%
1987	–	3.57%
1988	–	3.50%
1989	–	3.13%
1990	–	3.66%
1991	–	2.93%
1992	–	2.84%
1993	–	2.70%
1994	–	2.87%
1995	–	2.30%
1996	–	2.01%
1997	–	1.60%
1998	–	1.32%

Source: S&P 500 Composite Dividend Yield

owned it, the price of her stock rose so that at the end of the year it was worth $11 per share. It also paid a dividend of 20 cents per share at the end of the year. If we simply look at the change in price for the year, we can see that Joan's stock gained 10 percent ([$110 - $100] ÷ 100). However, when the 20 cents per share dividend is taken into account, her gain for the year was actually 12 percent ([$112 - $100] ÷ $100).

The fact that equity indexed annuities are not generally credited with dividends is an important fact that must be explained to clients. As noted in Chapter 3, dividends have traditionally contributed about 2 percent to 4 percent annually to the overall performance of the S&P 500. However, as was also noted, this dividend yield in recent years has been at an historical low point. Though the compounding of dividends can certainly add up over time, the fact that most EIAs do not reflect dividends is probably less of an issue currently than it would be if the dividend rate were high. Though practitioners must disclose to prospective buyers that EIAs that are linked to the S&P 500 do not include dividends, they can point out that this is a trade-off for the guarantee of principal EIAs provide. Most buyers, if they are qualified EIA prospects to begin with, will find this trade-off acceptable.

The consumer who purchases an equity indexed annuity is risk averse, either all the time or simply for that portion of his or her savings that is invested in the product. He or she can certainly invest in products that pass through the full dividend yield of the underlying securities. However, he or she will also get a pass-through of all the downside market risk. That risk, to some, is simply unacceptable.

Holding Periods

Some would argue that holding registered investments like stocks or indexed mutual funds for a long period of time will eventually overcome any short-term losses the market might experience. Studies certainly support this. The problem, however, is that many people do not hold these instruments long enough to take advantage of the potentially better long-term yields. A study conducted a few years ago by DALBAR, Inc., a financial research firm, indicated that, on average, investors who purchase no-load mutual funds hold them for only two years before moving their funds elsewhere. Load funds fared slightly better—they were held, on average, for four years.

By its design, the equity indexed annuity encourages the client to "stay the course" for at least the full term of the contract. This will support the full potential the product offers. However, due to the long-term nature of the EIA, the practitioner should determine whether or not the holding period the contract requires might present a problem for any earlier liquidity need the client might have that could force a surrender or withdrawal. Additionally, the practitioner should make sure the client realizes that any withdrawal from an annuity prior to the owner's age 59½ could be subject to a 10 percent early distribution penalty.

Participation Rates and Averaging

When EIAs were first introduced, there was a tendency to compare different contracts based upon the level of the participation rates. If a 50 percent participation rate was good, then a 75 percent participation rate must be better. However, just as attempts to compare declared-rate annuities only on the basis of initial interest rates can lead to inaccurate assumptions about the desirability of the product, so too can this type of comparison with EIAs.

When evaluating the participation rate of a particular product—let's say 75 percent, for example—one must ask the question, "Seventy-five percent of *what*?" It is only by looking at the participation rate in conjunction with the formula the insurer uses to measure changes in the index that one can fully understand the significance of the participation rate. To appreciate this, let's look at two different products.

Comparing Participation Rates: An Example

EIA Product A is a seven-year, point-to-point design with a 70 percent participation rate; EIA Product B is a seven-year, point-to-point design with a 75 percent participation rate. (It is important to limit any comparison to similarly designed products with similar terms. Annual resets will operate differently than high water marks, which will operate differently than point-to-point designs, etc.) Product A's interest crediting formula reflects the change in the S&P 500 Index value from the issue date of the contract—March 23, 1998—to the end of the term—March 23, seven years later. (These hypothetical values are shown in Ill. 8.2.)

ILL. 8.2 ■ *Hypothetical Index Values*

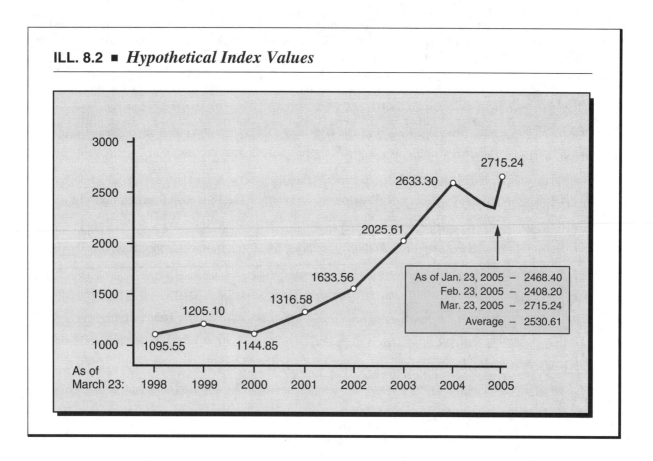

Let's assume Andy invested $10,000 in Product A:

Product A—70 Percent Participation Rate; $10,000 Premium

Index Value as of March 23, 1998: 1095.55

Index Value as of March 23, 2005: 2715.24

$$\text{Interest credited} = \frac{2715.24 - 1095.55}{1095.55} \times .70 = 103.49\%, \text{ or } \$10,349$$

Product B's interest crediting formula reflects the change in the S&P 500 Index value from the date of the contract's issue to the end of the seven-year term, but it averages the last three months' daily index values to arrive at that end value. Let's assume Bob invested $10,000 in Product B:

Product B—75 Percent Participation Rate; $10,000 Premium

Index Value as of March 23, 1998: 1095.55

Index Value (Averaged) as of March 23, 2005: 2530.61

$$\text{Interest credited} = \frac{2530.61 - 1095.55}{1095.55} \times .75 = 98.24\%, \text{ or } \$9,824$$

As we can see, Bob's 75 percent participation rate in Product B actually resulted in less interest credited to his contract than Andy's 70 percent participation rate with Product A. Due to the fact that the index was rising steadily toward the end of the contract term, the averaging feature in Product B lowered the overall interest credited despite the higher participation rate.

On the other hand, had the index fallen sharply toward the end of the contract term, the averaging feature of Product B would have protected Bob from such a drop and Product B would have credited more interest than Product A.

An averaging feature included in an EIA can be considered a positive or a negative. As the above example illustrates, averaging in an indexing formula takes into account more days of index performance. Most often used in the final year of a point-to-point product, averaging reduces the influence of the index's value on the final day of the term. Though averaging has some inherent benefits, it can also have a negative effect on the amount of interest a contract holder might earn in an EIA. Following are the most frequently cited advantages and disadvantages of averaging:

Advantages	*Disadvantages*
• Provides protection from end-of-year or end-of-term declines, if averaging occurs at end of year or end of term	• Limits interest earnings potential, slightly if index is moving up slowly, more drastically if index moves up in a straight line
• Lowers the risk of purchasing the EIA at a "peak" level if averaging occurs at the beginning of the term	
• Minimizes volatility by lessening the effects on interest credits of any extreme highs or lows in the index	

As one might infer from the above, the value—or drawback—of averaging depends a great deal on how risk-averse a client might be. No one can predict with certainty which direction the stock market or a stock market index will take. Therefore, the perceived value of averaging to a given client depends on how he or she feels about risk in general and the events described above specifically.

Interest Caps

A cap applied to an equity indexed annuity is the maximum interest rate that will be credited to the contract, regardless of the actual interest rate the crediting formula produces. As with other features inherent to an EIA, it represents a trade-off for the guarantees the product offers. It too must be viewed in conjunction with all the other aspects of the product before any conclusion can be drawn regarding its beneficial or negative significance. Following are the most often noted advantages and disadvantages of capping interest:

Advantages	*Disadvantages*
• May allow the insurance carrier to offer other design advantages such as annual interest crediting, liquidity, compounding of interest and/or higher participation rates	• Limits the amount of interest that the client can earn
• Risk averse clients (or those who would otherwise invest only in fixed interest rate vehicles) may not object to a cap, provided it is higher than what they might achieve on other fixed interest products	• Insurer retains control over if and when the cap is changed and how high or low it will be (possibly subject to some overall limits stated in the contract)
	• An annual lock-in of interest, liquidity and/or compounding of interest can be achieved *without* capping interest, possibly at the expense of a lower participation rate or other features

In light of the above, the practitioner should ask the client how he or she feels about a cap on interest earned. Certainly, for contracts that do impose a cap, the practitioner should look for other features that would provide a benefit for buyers.

Simple vs. Compound Interest

An EIA design will provide either simple interest or compound interest. In a simple interest design, interest does not earn interest; the earnings throughout the term are simply added together to produce the total interest earned. In a compound interest design, interest earnings from previous years will earn current interest. In either case, regardless of how interest is calculated on a year-by-year basis, the interest earned during the entire term typically compounds when a new term begins. For example, assume Product A is an annual reset simple interest design. It calculates changes in the index each year and applies the participation rate to the result. The interest earned each year is added together over the first seven years of the term. At the end of the seventh year, the client decides to renew the contract for another seven years. New interest earned will be calculated based on the contract's total value from the end of year seven. Thus, there is some element of compounding in this design, albeit limited. Product B is a compound interest design. New interest each year will be calculated based on the total contract value from the end of the prior year. All other product features being equal, Product B will always produce more interest than Product A.

On the surface, it certainly appears that a client would never want anything other than compound interest. However, the value of compound interest in an EIA design may be mitigated by other contract factors and features. It is common, for example, for products that compound interest to impose a cap on interest earnings. Conversely, a contract that does not contain a compound interest function may have other features a client deems important. Or, the compounded product may contain a design element that dilutes the value of its compound interest and which could, ultimately, result in the crediting of *less* interest than a simple interest design. Again, it is a matter of knowing and explaining all of a product's features that will help clients determine a design that makes the most sense to them.

Surrender Charges

Some EIA products contain a surrender charge schedule that assesses specific charges upon withdrawals or surrenders. Other contracts may not contain an explicit surrender charge schedule; instead, they might provide for loss of earnings if the client withdraws funds or surrenders early. This loss of earnings may be implicit in the contract's definition of "surrender value." For example, an EIA might define "surrender value" as equal to the guaranteed minimum contract value, which would typically be 3 percent compounded annually on 90 percent of the initial premium. Thus, if the contract were surrendered before the end of the term, the owner would lose all index-linked interest—quite a penalty, and possibly more severe than any charges that an explicit surrender schedule might impose.

The same caution applies to any partial withdrawal provisions a contract may contain. In some contracts, even though there is no explicit surrender charge imposed on withdrawals, there may be a loss of all interest credited to the amount of the withdrawal. Again, the practitioner must review the contract language carefully to ensure that he or she understands the withdrawal provisions and can explain them properly to the client.

Evaluate the Full Contract

As the preceding review indicates, the practitioner must look at *all* facets of an EIA contract when evaluating its features and benefits. A contract's interest crediting formula, for example, cannot be defined only in terms of its participation rate. Averaging, caps, vesting schedules and whether or not interest is compounded will all affect the formula. Furthermore, a particular contract feature that may be considered a disadvantage by one client may not be an issue at all for another—it all depends on what the client desires and to what extent a given product can help meet his or her goals.

■ PRODUCT DESIGN BEHAVIOR

Fundamental to the process of evaluating an EIA contract is assessing an EIA's basic design chassis and determining which will be best for the client. Annual reset? Point-to-point? High water mark? Low water mark? Each of these designs is unique and each will perform differently in different types of market environments. If we ignore specific product features for a moment and simply look at basic product designs, the following charts and explanations should be helpful.

Point-to-Point Design

The point-to-point method will credit the most interest when the index is rising steadily. Specifically, a point-to-point design will credit more interest than a high water mark or an annual reset design when the index is rising and not experiencing much downside movement. The advantages of the point-to-point design are that it is simple to explain, it usually offers a higher participation rate than other product designs and there is usually no cap imposed on interest earnings.

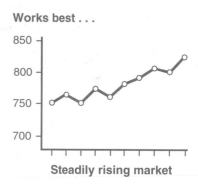

Works best . . .

Steadily rising market

On the other hand, point-to-point designs have some inherent disadvantages. The interest crediting formula looks at only two points to calculate interest earnings: the beginning point and the end point. If the index drops sharply on the last day of the term, the client's interest earnings would be significantly affected. Furthermore, with this type of design there is typically limited liquidity and, if the funds are removed during the term—due to annuitization, death or surrender—the contract may not provide for indexed values, but only guaranteed values.

High Water Mark

The high water mark design does well in many environments, but credits the most interest (relative to the point-to-point and annual reset designs) when the index reaches a high early or in the middle of the contract's term, followed by a steady fall thereafter.

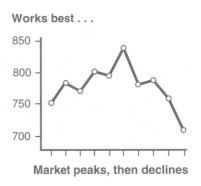

Works best . . .

Market peaks, then declines

The advantage of the high water mark design is that more than the beginning and ending index values are taken into consideration in the interest crediting formula. Five to seven days throughout the term (typically on contract anniversaries) are reviewed in order to determine the high point. The participation rate on a high water mark is usually guaranteed for the entire term of the contract, and indexed values are generally available for annuitization, death and surrender. The disadvantage of the high water market design is that there may be a cap on interest earnings and a lower participation rate relative to some other designs. There may also be explicit surrender charges or a vesting schedule.

Annual Reset

The annual reset design works best in a very volatile market with a lot of fluctuation. It will credit significantly more interest than the high water mark and annual reset designs when the index fluctuates a lot during the term, but does not end up too far from where it started when the contract was purchased. The distinct advantage of the annual reset design is that the client's interest earnings are locked in each and every year; they are never affected by subsequent decreases in the index. In essence, the client is "in" for the up years and "out" for the down years. (In years where the interest crediting formula would produce a negative result, the client receives 0 percent interest.)

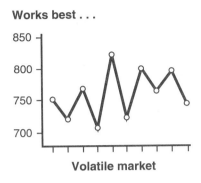

Works best . . .

Volatile market

Also, the annual starting point for calculating changes in the index is reset each year. If the S&P 500 value was 890 when John purchased his annual reset EIA, and it ended up at 700 one year later, all new growth in the next year—contract year two—would be measured from the lower S&P 500 value of 700. As has been noted, some of the best years of index performance occur in the "recovery period" after a down year. The annual reset design takes advantage of this market behavior.

The annual reset design typically makes indexed values available each year if the client annuitizes, dies, withdraws or surrenders early (contrasted to those designs that only make guaranteed values available for these events). However, the possible disadvantages to the annual reset design include the fact that participation rates or margins may change annually and there may be a cap on interest.

Low Water Mark

Much like the high water mark, the low water mark works well in a number of different environments. The difference is that the LWM performs best in a market that declines precipitously early on then rises throughout the remainder of the term. It does not perform well in a market that declines early and stays down.

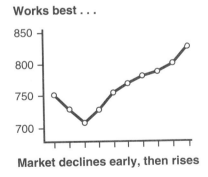

Works best . . .

Market declines early, then rises

Like the high water mark design, the advantage of a LWM product is that more than the beginning and ending index values are taken into consideration in the interest crediting formula. Several days throughout the term (typically on contract anniversaries) are taken into account in order to determine the low point.

Multi-Year Reset

Products using a multi-year reset work well in a highly volatile market, especially if the peaks and valleys coincide with the reset points. This approach performs the worst in a steadily rising market with low volatility.

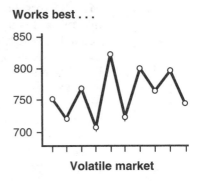

Works best . . .

Volatile market

Digital

This methodology works best in a market that rises slightly each year. It works the worst in a market that alternates downturns with large upswings.

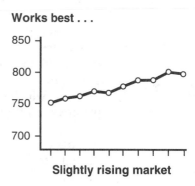

Works best . . .

Slightly rising market

■ UNDERSTANDING HISTORICAL INTEREST CREDITING

Understanding EIA designs and features is only part of the story. Also required is a general idea of the interest crediting *potential* these products may have. Just as a diligent practitioner would not sell a declared-rate annuity without examining the insurance company's renewal rate policies and history, he or she should have an understanding of how an EIA might credit interest in different types of market environments. The stock market and stock market indexes can go up, but obviously they can also go down. Though the last 15 years have proven to be (mostly) a period of exceptional stock market returns, the practitioner needs to establish realistic expectations with his or her clients regarding the interest crediting potential of an EIA in future years. The best way to do this would be to examine historical behavior. The problem is that modern EIAs have been around for a relatively short period of time. There is, therefore, very little historical behavior to refer to.

At the time of this book's publication, insurance industry regulatory organizations were still struggling to devise a standardized way of providing consumers with information regarding EIAs' future interest crediting potential. Due to the many variances in product designs, it has been difficult to create a methodology that is, first, fair to all products and, second, simple for consumers to understand. As a minimum level of disclosure, many insurers voluntarily provide information that shows what would have been the best and worst historical time periods for their products and how much interest would have been credited to the products during those time periods. One of the problems with this approach is that insurers typically use the participation rates or margins that are in effect *today* and assume they were at the same level historically. This is an unrealistic assumption.

Many factors, both macroeconomic and microeconomic, help determine participation rates. It is unlikely that these factors would have remained static over many years. For instance, commission levels and profits—examples of microeconomic factors—are not the same today as they were years ago, nor are call option prices or bond interest rates, which are macroeconomic factors. Unfortunately, we cannot accurately reconstruct macroeconomic conditions of the past; for example, we do not know what S&P 500 call options would have cost 20 years ago because they did not exist back then. And we are only able to partially reconstruct microeconomic conditions. The only history that can be accurately reconstructed is past interest rates. To this extent, participation rates and margins can be adjusted to reflect historical interest rate environments. For this purpose, the interest rate of choice would be the 10-year Treasury note rate since its duration most closely matches the term of most indexed products.

Any historically-adjusted participation rates or margins will not be perfect, but the results they yield and the interest crediting they reflect are likely to be more accurate than the results that unadjusted participation rates and margins would yield. They will also help the practitioner understand the relationship between bond interest rates (which back the minimum interest guarantees of the EIA) and the participation rates offered on various product designs.

Illustrations 8.3 and 8.4 show how an annual reset product design might have credited interest historically in an "up," "down" and "average" market environment. Since the underlying index for most EIAs today is the S&P 500, it is valid and useful for educational purposes to contrast the product with the S&P 500's performance during the same time period as the term of the annuity. Illustration 8.3 reflects historical interest crediting without adjustment to the participation rate; Illustration 8.4 shows interest crediting with an adjusted participation rate. (The assumptions used for both are detailed at the end of this chapter.)

Illustration 8.3: Unadjusted Participation Rate

Illustration 8.3 shows how a seven-year annual reset annuity with a 60 percent participation rate and a 14 percent cap would have performed during the periods 1982 through 1992 (an "up" market); 1964 through 1974 (a "down" market); and 1958 through 1968 (an "average" market). In each of the three scenarios, Column 1 shows the actual annual return of the S&P 500 during these years. It is an important measure in that it allows us to see the actual fluctuations in the market as they occur each year, providing a view of just how much volatility the market incurs over time. It also provides additional insight into the benefits of the EIA that provide protection from such volatility.

Column 2 shows the hypothetical interest credited to the annuity for the seven-year rolling time periods, expressed as an annualized rate. In other words, using the "up" market as an example, the four rates shown—9.16 percent, 7.14 percent, 8.33 percent and 7.83 percent—indicate the hypothetical annualized interest the contract would have earned, assuming issue dates of 8/12/82, 8/12/83, 8/12/84 and 8/12/85. The reason an annualized rate is shown is to reflect common industry practice of putting all types of financial products on a "level playing field" when comparing yield or performance. It would be misleading to try to compare two financial products that touted a 30 percent return and a 10 percent return, respectively. The 30 percent return may have been achieved over a five-year period while the 10 percent

ILL. 8.3 ■ *Unadjusted Participation Rate*

ABC Life Insurance Co. 7-Year Annual Reset Annuity
60 Percent Participation Rate, 14 Percent Interest Cap

Scenario 1: *Up Market   08/12/82 – 08/12/92*

1 S&P 500 Annual Return		2 Annual Reset EIA Annualized Return	3 Annual Reset EIA Total Return	4 S&P 500 Annualized (Over EIA Contract Term)	5 S&P 500 Total Return (Over EIA Contract Term)
8/12/83	58.33%				
8/12/84	2.01%				
8/12/85	13.43%				
8/12/86	29.69%				
8/12/87	36.59%				
8/12/88	−21.01%				
8/12/89	31.30%	9.16%	84.70%	18.93%	236.56%
8/12/90	− 2.67%	7.14%	62.00%	10.95%	106.93%
8/12/91	15.65%	8.33%	75.10%	12.95%	134.56%
8/12/92	7.67%	7.83%	69.50%	12.11%	122.63%

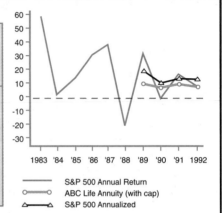

S&P 500 Annual Return
ABC Life Annuity (with cap)
S&P 500 Annualized

Scenario 2: *Down Market   11/30/64 – 11/30/74*

1 S&P 500 Annual Return		2 Annual Reset EIA Annualized Return	3 Annual Reset EIA Total Return	4 S&P 500 Annualized (Over EIA Contract Term)	5 S&P 500 Total Return (Over EIA Contract Term)
11/30/65	8.52%				
11/30/66	−12.18%				
11/30/67	16.84%				
11/30/68	15.29%				
11/30/69	−13.44%				
11/30/70	− 7.05%				
11/30/71	7.79%	4.07%	32.21%	1.55%	11.37%
11/30/72	24.13%	5.29%	43.45%	3.51%	27.31%
11/30/73	−17.75%	5.29%	43.45%	2.55%	19.28%
11/30/74	−27.08%	3.85%	30.27%	−4.13%	−25.56%

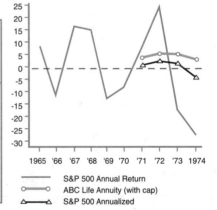

S&P 500 Annual Return
ABC Life Annuity (with cap)
S&P 500 Annualized

Scenario 3: *Average Market   10/30/58 – 10/30/68*

1 S&P 500 Annual Return		2 Annual Reset EIA Annualized Return	3 Annual Reset EIA Total Return	4 S&P 500 Annualized (Over EIA Contract Term)	5 S&P 500 Total Return (Over EIA Contract Term)
10/30/59	12.19%				
10/30/60	− 7.15%				
10/30/61	28.10%				
10/30/62	−17.36%				
10/30/63	30.53%				
10/30/64	14.99%				
10/30/65	8.91%	6.96%	60.16%	8.78%	80.24%
10/30/66	−13.18%	5.88%	49.18%	4.87%	39.50%

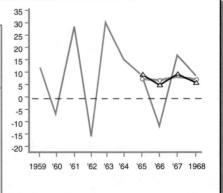

return may have been achieved in the previous quarter. The only way to adequately compare the performance of two or more financial products is to view them over the same period of time and break their total returns down into a constant annual rate of return. Therefore, what Column 2 shows is the level, unchanging interest rate that the EIA contract would have earned annually and compounded annually to produce the total interest that would have actually been credited to this annuity at the end of its seven-year term.

Column 3 shows the total interest earned on the annuity contract for each of the seven-year rolling time periods, reflecting the participation rate and the floor.

Columns 4 and 5 show, respectively, the annualized return of the S&P 500 and the total return of the S&P 500 over the same term as the annuity. In essence, these columns present the S&P 500 as if it were a seven-year annual reset EIA. The figures in these columns bring home the point of how the minimum guarantees of this annual reset annuity—both the 0 percent floor and the guaranteed minimum return—protect the contract owner during years the market is down. If we look at "Scenario 2—Down Market," we can see that the EIA's guarantees helped provide interest crediting that was higher than that which would have been achieved by a seven-year investment in the S&P 500 itself. Especially noteworthy is the fact that a contract that reached the end of its seven-year term on November 30, 1974, would have achieved a positive 3.85 percent annualized interest rate and total interest of 30.27 percent when an investment in the S&P 500 would have experienced a *negative* annualized return of –4.13 percent and a *negative* total return of –25.56 percent. This drives home one of the chief benefits of the equity indexed annuity.

Illustration 8.4: Adjusted Participation Rate

Illustration 8.4 reflects the differences in EIA interest crediting that can occur—sometimes dramatic, sometimes not—when the participation rate is *adjusted* based on what the interest rate environment was for the period shown. Recall from previous discussions that one of the insurer's costs of backing its EIA product is the cost of purchasing bonds to cover the contract's minimum guarantee. The cost of bonds goes up or down based upon where market interest rates are at that time. If interest rates are up, the price of bonds is lower; therefore, less money needs to be spent on bonds and more money can be spent on the call options that back the indexed interest crediting component of the contract. Under these circumstances, participation rates would move up. Conversely, if interest rates are down, more money must be spent on bonds, less money would be available for call options and participation rates would go down. Consequently, the interest rate environment—which would be different in up, down and average markets—directly affects participation rates. This is what Ill. 8.4 reflects. The product shown is the same as in Ill. 8.3: a seven-year annual reset design, but with its participation rate adjusted for the same market periods.

As the examples show, it is possible to make some approximations of how a particular EIA will credit interest in various market environments. However, due to the fact that the historical results in these examples are hypothetical in nature, they cannot be presented to clients as illustrations. The practitioner must keep in mind that potential interest crediting is only one component of the EIA sale. All of the other features and benefits of the product must make sense to the client. We will soon discuss this issue in greater detail as it relates to market conduct.

ILL. 8.4 ■ *Adjusted Participation Rate*

ABC Life Insurance Co. 7-Year Annual Reset Annuity

Scenario 1: *Up Market 08/12/82 – 08/12/92*

1 S&P 500 Annual Return		2 Annual Reset EIA Annualized Return	3 Annual Reset EIA Total Return	4 S&P 500 Annualized (Over EIA Contract Term)	5 S&P 500 Total Return (Over EIA Contract Term)
8/12/83	58.33%				
8/12/84	2.01%				
8/12/85	13.43%				
8/12/86	29.69%				
8/12/87	36.59%				
8/12/88	−21.01%				
8/12/89	31.30%	10.25%	98.00%	18.93%	236.56%
8/12/90	− 2.67%	8.18%	73.39%	10.95%	106.93%
8/12/91	15.65%	9.81%	92.53%	12.95%	134.56%
8/12/92	7.67%	9.13%	84.34%	12.11%	122.63%

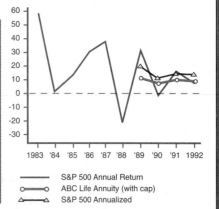

S&P 500 Annual Return
ABC Life Annuity (with cap)
S&P 500 Annualized

Scenario 2: *Down Market 11/30/64 – 11/30/74*

1 S&P 500 Annual Return		2 Annual Reset EIA Annualized Return	3 Annual Reset EIA Total Return	4 S&P 500 Annualized (Over EIA Contract Term)	5 S&P 500 Total Return (Over EIA Contract Term)
11/30/65	8.52%				
11/30/66	−12.18%				
11/30/67	16.84%				
11/30/68	15.29%				
11/30/69	−13.44%				
11/30/70	− 7.05%				
11/30/71	7.79%	2.50%	18.87%	1.55%	11.37%
11/30/72	24.13%	3.71%	29.06%	3.51%	27.31%
11/30/73	−17.75%	4.42%	35.36%	2.55%	19.28%
11/30/74	−27.08%	3.86%	30.36%	−4.13%	−25.56%

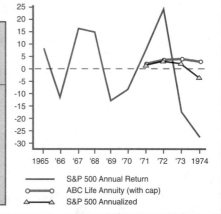

S&P 500 Annual Return
ABC Life Annuity (with cap)
S&P 500 Annualized

Scenario 3: *Average Market 10/30/58 – 10/30/68*

1 S&P 500 Annual Return		2 Annual Reset EIA Annualized Return	3 Annual Reset EIA Total Return	4 S&P 500 Annualized (Over EIA Contract Term)	5 S&P 500 Total Return (Over EIA Contract Term)
10/30/59	12.19%				
10/30/60	− 7.15%				
10/30/61	28.10%				
10/30/62	−17.36%				
10/30/63	30.53%				
10/30/64	14.99%				
10/30/65	8.91%	3.91%	30.80%	8.78%	80.24%
10/30/66	−13.18%	4.40%	35.18%	4.87%	39.50%
10/30/67	18.13%	4.44%	35.54%	8.54%	77.47%
10/30/68	8.98%	3.67%	28.70%	6.06%	50.96%

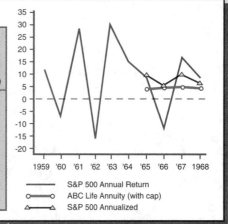

S&P 500 Annual Return
ABC Life Annuity (with cap)
S&P 500 Annualized

The source for the examples in these illustrations is IPOD™, Index Products on Disk, copyright NFC Consulting Group.

■ THE ELUSIVE "PERFECT PRODUCT"

As we have seen, it is important to understand the effect that different EIA product features such as averaging, caps and participation rates have on interest crediting. It is also helpful to take a look at historical interest crediting behavior, albeit subject to the limitations described earlier. When all is said and done, however, the easiest way for the practitioner to determine which clients would be good candidates for EIAs and to get some clues as to what type of EIA would be the best choice is to develop a client profile. To do so, the practitioner should ask the following questions:

Question #1:
What type of client will I be speaking to?

- Is the client conservative and risk averse, or does he or she understand and accept risk/reward?

- Is the client financially savvy or financially unsophisticated?

- Does the client own (or not own) stocks or other registered securities like mutual funds or variable annuities?

- Does the client have a long-term or short-term savings horizon?

- Does the client have or not have a need for liquidity?

- Is the client concerned or not concerned about:

  - the current amount of taxes he or she pays?

  - the estate value left for heirs?

  - probate?

  - outliving his or her income in retirement?

The bottom line is this: Would this client benefit by owning a fixed annuity *regardless* of the equity-linked interest feature? If so, the practitioner has a potential equity index annuity buyer to talk to.

Question #2:
What expectations do I (and my client) have regarding the level of the S&P 500 during the years the annuity would be held?

- Will it climb?
  (If so, point-to-point design will work well.)

- Will it rise for a while, then decline?
  (If so, high water mark design will work well.)

- Will it go up and down a lot—a "bumpy" ride?
  (If so, annual or multi-year reset design will work well.)

- Will it decline drastically but trend up from a low point?
  (If so, low water mark will work well.)

- Will it rise slightly each year with no drastic declines?
  (If so, digital will work well.)

To this question, the practitioner and client may prudently say, "I have no idea." That is why it is important to view the equity index annuity as just one part of a client's well diversified retirement portfolio. A well-diversified portfolio promotes the likelihood that if one segment or product is not experiencing growth, another is. However, if the practitioner is addressing a client who has strong feelings about the direction of the market or the index, it is certainly appropriate to provide him or her with a choice that has the *potential* to offer the best possible interest in that scenario (as long as the other product features suit the client's needs as well).

Question #3:
How well do I understand the product I am considering presenting?
Can I easily explain all of its features in a manner that is perfectly clear to the client?

It's trite but true—don't sell what you or your client must struggle to understand.

No financial product on the market today can be all things to all people and the EIA is no exception. Each design has its own advantages and disadvantages. The role of the practitioner is to help clients make informed choices.

■ MARKET CONDUCT ISSUES

As with any financial product, the practitioner is expected to utilize good market conduct when offering equity indexed annuities to consumers. Due to their unique nature, EIAs may require some special care when they are being discussed in a sales presentation.

Emphasize Traditional Fixed Annuity Features and Benefits

The fact that its credited rate of interest is linked to an equity index is obviously a major aspect of the EIA's appeal. However, in client presentations, the practitioner should never overlook the traditional fixed annuity features and benefits that are also important to the conservative individual, such as guaranteed minimum interest, guarantee of principal, lifetime income potential through annuitization and death benefit. These features are the very foundation upon which any fixed annuity sale is built. In fact, as noted in Chapter 1, the "safe harbor" rule for annuities requires that the marketing of the "insurance" attributes of these products be primary to any investment-related features or benefits.

ILL. 8.5 ■ *Do's and Don'ts of Equity Indexed Annuity Compliance*

Do . . .

- Refer to the S&P 500 Index as one of the factors that helps determine the interest rate
- Describe the product as a long-term retirement savings vehicle
- Emphasize that the product is designed as an appropriate planning vehicle for retirement security
- Emphasize the guarantees, including the guaranteed minimum interest rate and the guaranteed principal
- Emphasize the product's insurance benefits, including the death benefit and annuitization options
- Explain the indexing feature and be clear as to whether the participation rate, margin or any other component of the indexing formula can change during the initial term or subsequent terms
- Explain that the S&P 500 Index does not reflect dividends
- Be clear that the entity backing the product's guarantees is an insurance company
- Use the term "equity" in conjunction with "linked" or "indexed"
- Market the product as a fixed annuity product
- Stress protection from index declines and/or market loss

Don't . . .

- Use investment terms such as "stock market," "investing in the contract," "performance," "investment returns" and "Wall Street" except with extreme care and appropriate caveats
- Describe the EIA's indexing feature, or formula, as a means of "direct participation" in the stock market, the equity markets or the S&P 500 Index
- Provide a list—complete or partial—of the stocks or companies that comprise the S&P 500 or any other index unless it is explained within the context of describing what the index is
- Compare an EIA product to a registered product
- Use standard equity market terminology to describe an EIA
- Refer to securities unless it is to contrast their features to those of an EIA
- Use sales material that is not approved by the insurer backing the EIA
- Focus on the indexed interest features without providing balanced commentary on other fixed annuity features, such as the guaranteed minimum interest rate, income options, guaranteed principal, probate efficiency, etc.

Contrast (Do Not Compare) EIAs to Investment Products

Though it may be tempting to compare the EIA to investment products to show how they might be better for a client, this is entirely inappropriate. Registered products cannot be compared to nonregistered products or vice versa. Nor can the practitioner focus primarily or exclusively on certain product features to the exclusion of others. Admittedly, not being able to compare the EIA to an investment product can pose something of a dilemma. There are probably many more consumers today who are more familiar with mutual funds and the stock market than they are with annuities and it may be natural for some to want a comparison of the EIA to various investment products. In these instances, the key to good market conduct is to reinforce how the EIA *differs* from a security. Registered securities products provide full participation in market gains, with the associated full participation in market losses. There is no guarantee of principal. Additionally, registered securities products can be purchased for either long- or short-term investing. EIAs are purchased primarily by consumers who have long-term accumulation of retirement savings as their goal.

Know the Product(s) You Represent and Any Trade-offs They Entail

There is no such thing as a "perfect product." The practitioner must be able and willing to discuss design trade-offs with clients—what the client must give up in one area to achieve in another. This would include, for instance, an annual lock-in-of-interest feature, which may be offset by a cap on earnings, or a higher participation rate, which is offset by averaging. For specific designs, certain features need to be explained carefully. Clients who are interested in an annual reset design, for example, need to understand that in years when the performance of the index would cause a negative interest result, the percentage of interest credited will be 0. Inherently, this is one of the benefits of the EIA because it protects the client from loss of interest. However, some conservative fixed income investors are accustomed to receiving interest each and every year on their bonds or CDs. The mechanics of the EIA differ, and, therefore, further explanation may be required.

At a minimum, the kind of information the practitioner should be able and prepared to provide to prospective EIA buyers is represented by the following questions. These questions appear in the National Association of Insurance Commissioners' *Buyer's Guide to Equity Indexed Annuities* as questions the consumer should ask the agent or the insurer:

1. What is the guaranteed minimum interest rate?

2. What charges, if any, are deducted from my premium?

3. What charges, if any, are deducted from my contract value?

4. How long is the term?

5. What is the participation rate?

6. For how long is the participation rate guaranteed?

7. Is there a minimum participation rate?

8. Does my contract have a cap?

9. Is averaging used? How does it work?

10. Is interest compounded during a term?

11. Is there a margin, spread or administrative fee? Is that in addition to or instead of a participation rate?

12. Which indexing method is used in my contract?

13. What are the surrender charges or penalties if I want to end my contract early and take out all of my money?

14. Can I get a partial withdrawal without paying charges or losing interest? Does my contract have vesting?

15. Does my annuity waive withdrawal charges if I am confined to a nursing home or diagnosed with a terminal illness?

16. What annuity income payment options do I have?

17. What is the death benefit?

Understand What You Are Selling

When all is said and done, the best product to recommend to a client is the one that the practitioner understands inside and out and can easily explain. Due care should be taken to review not only sales material but also any formal disclosure notices provided to the client as well as the policy form. Most insurance companies today make a wide variety of training materials available to practitioners marketing their products. The practitioner owes it to his or her clients to be as knowledgeable as possible about any financial product he or she recommends.

■ SUMMARY

The primary objective of *Equity Indexed Annuities* is to provide the practitioner with the necessary information to be able to evaluate the EIA and its potential place in a client's long-term savings and accumulation plan. It is the authors' hope that the text has provided an understanding of the mechanics of the equity indexed annuity that will enable him or her to perform such an evaluation. Only when one is completely comfortable with the concept of the EIA can its benefits be explained to potential buyers.

The equity indexed annuity market is new and exciting, offering much potential to practitioners who sell these unique products. Certainly EIAs are destined to evolve and change in the coming years; for those who embrace these products, there will be the constant responsibility to seek out new information as it becomes available in order to serve and educate their clients in the best manner possible.

■ CHAPTER REVIEW QUESTIONS

1. Which of the following is NOT typical of a point-to-point EIA design?

   A. It usually offers a higher participation rate than other product designs.
   B. A cap on interest earnings is a typical contract provision.
   C. It performs best in a steadily rising market.
   D. It is easily explained to clients.

2. Which of the following would NOT be proper market conduct when presenting an EIA to a consumer?

A. Emphasizing the product's traditional fixed annuity features and benefits

B. Pointing out the trade-offs the product entails

C. Comparing the EIA to registered investment products

D. Explaining that the consumer's principal is guaranteed against market risk

3. The effect of an averaging feature in an EIA design is to minimize the effects on interest credits of either extreme highs or extreme lows in the index.

True or False

4. It is considered improper market conduct to point out that while interest credited to EIAs does not reflect dividends, this can be considered a trade-off for the guarantee of principal the products provide.

True or False

Assumptions Used For Historical Interest Crediting Scenarios

The source for the examples in the scenarios on pages 109 and 111 is Index Products on Disk (IPOD™), developed by NFC Consulting Group.

Average Market The average market was derived as follows:

1. The annual return of the S&P 500 was calculated on a daily basis, starting with its inception on March 4, 1957 through December 31, 1997.

2. Next, the average annual return from the population derived in #1 was calculated. This is the *historical average return*.

3. In addition, the standard deviation of the population derived in #1 was calculated. This is the *historical standard deviation*.

   S&P 500, 3/5/57–12/31/97:

   Historical average return: 8.94%
   Historical standard deviation: 15.30%

4. Looking at 10-year periods, 10-year average annual returns that were within 20 basis points, plus or minus, of the historical average were selected.

5. Using those 10-year periods derived in #4, the data was further refined to select 10-year periods with standard deviations closest to the standard deviation of the population.

   Average Market, 10/30/58–10/30/68

   Average return: 8.85%
   Standard deviation: 15.30%

Up Market

The up market was derived as follows:

1. The annual return of the S&P 500 was calculated on a daily basis, from March 4, 1957 through December 31, 1997.

2. From this, the sum total of 10 years of annual returns on a daily basis was calculated.

3. The maximum 10-year return value for all of the 10-year periods was identified. This period was selected as the "up market."

   Up Market, 8/12/82–8/12/92

   Average return: 17.02%

Down Market

The down market was derived as follows:

1. The 10-year returns derived in Step 2 of the up market calculations were also used to calculate the down market.

2. The minimum 10-year return value for all of the 10-year periods was calculated to produce the "down market."

   Down Market, 11/30/64–11/30/74

   Average return: −1.89%

Interest Earnings Calculations

The following assumptions were made in order to facilitate the demonstration of the product's interest earnings calculation:

1. Only the initial term was used. Note: For flexible products, it is assumed that only a single premium payment is received during the term and the participation rate does not change during the term.

2. No withdrawals were made.

3. Accumulated values were based on a single premium only.

4. Participation rate did not change within the term.

5. Premium taxes have not been taken into account.

Adjusted Participation Rates

In general, participation rates (and margins) are based primarily on the cost of bonds, the cost of options and other financial and competitive factors. The calculation of the adjusted participation rates was based only on current and historical yields-to-maturities on 10-year Treasury notes because historical information is not available for the cost of options and other factors. The 10-year Treasury note rate was utilized because its duration most closely matches the term of most index products.

Common Questions Practitioners Ask About EIAs

- *Can't a client achieve the same objectives with a variable annuity?*

Not really. The investment of premium dollars into a variable annuity's (VA) subaccounts means that the contract holder assumes market risk. EIAs do not have market risk. In up markets, EIAs tend to underperform variable annuities but will outperform VAs in down markets or highly volatile markets. Even if a VA owner divided his or her money between the general account and the subaccounts, the portion allocated to the subaccounts is still subject to risk. Over long periods of time, a variable annuity invested in this fashion could outperform an EIA, but the year-by-year volatility that is inherent to the subaccounts may be an issue with a conservative client. Due to the market risk issue, the risk profiles of the VA buyer and of the EIA buyer are very different.

- *The only reason EIAs look so good right now is because the S&P 500 has produced incredible returns the past few years. What happens when the market drops?*

No one can predict with any certainty what the equity markets or an equity index will do in the future. However, for most clients, that would not be a good enough reason to avoid a product that has the potential to offer a higher rate of return than other types of fixed interest products. If the EIA is positioned correctly—if it is presented as a way to address part of a client's overall retirement strategy (as opposed to functioning as the entire solution)—downward market movements should not be cause for concern. The EIA should be just one aspect of a well-diversified financial strategy. Keep in mind why an individual purchases an EIA in the first place: *the potential to earn higher interest without market risk.* If the individual wants a steady (but conservative) interest rate at all times and in all market environments, the traditional declared-rate fixed annuity may be a better choice.

- *When's the best time to get into an EIA?*

It really doesn't matter whether the index is high or low when an EIA purchase is made; what matters is where the index goes from there. Since no one has been able to consistently predict this, there's no reason to believe anyone can now. In other words, no one knows where the index will go from here, which is a perfect reason to buy an EIA.

- *EIA products are so complicated. How can I explain them to my clients?*

Some EIA products certainly are complicated, but many are straightforward and some are downright simple to explain. You should choose a product that is easily understood by you and your clients.

- *Why doesn't the insurance company provide for compound interest?*

It's true that some insurers don't compound interest annually on their EIA products, though most do compound at the end of the term. Noncompounding is not necessarily the mark of an inferior product. When an insurer does not provide for compounding, it has likely incorporated another beneficial feature into the product's design. Look for more liquidity or a higher participation rate, for example.

- *Why don't EIAs offer greater liquidity?*

It's true that no EIA is designed for a great deal of ongoing liquidity during the initial term. Clients should be prepared to leave their funds undisturbed. For older clients who may have to meet minimum distribution requirements, a number of EIA designs do offer liquidity for this purpose.

- *The S&P 500 rose more than 30 percent in one year but my client received only 16 percent on his EIA. Should this bother me or my client?*

Neither you nor your client should be bothered—nor should you be surprised. The 16 percent return is a function of the EIA design that you sold. You should fully understand how the product is designed so you can coach your client along the way about what to expect. Virtually everyone would accept a 16 percent return from a vehicle that guarantees no downside risk, but no one likes surprises. As long as the representative is knowledgeable about the product, the client shouldn't experience any surprises.

- *Are EIAs variable annuities?*

The vast majority of EIAs are filed with state insurance departments as fixed annuities whereas variable annuities are registered with the SEC. Unlike VAs, EIAs comply with fixed annuity nonforfeiture regulations and are accepted by state insurance commissioners as fixed products. It is still possible that the SEC, which has the final word on what is and is not a security, will promulgate some sort of ruling in the future.

- *Which is better for my clients—a margin or a participation rate?*

Neither is better; they are simply different ways of accomplishing the same thing. However, it is true that margins tend to produce better interest crediting when index returns are high and participation rates are better if returns are low.

- *Is it better for the participation rate to be guaranteed for the initial term or allowed to float?*

Our research indicates that one reason EIA buyers like indexing is that the "trust me" aspect, which is inherent to traditional declared-rate annuities, is removed from the equation. EIA contracts that do not guarantee participation rates, allowing them to be subject to change each year, bring back the "trust me" concept. On the other hand, being able to change the participation rate lowers an insurer's risk, which would allow it to add other beneficial features to the product.

- *Point-to-point, high water, annual reset—which methodology is ultimately the best for the client?*

No one method is "best" nor is any one method better than another—they're just different. You should have an idea of the types of market environments that enhance the performance of the various methodologies, but ultimately, methods and products should be evaluated for ease of understanding and effectiveness in achieving a client's retirement goals.

- *Where do you position an EIA in an investment strategy?*

Keep in mind that an EIA is not really an investment product; it is a retirement *savings* product. This means it should be positioned as part of an overall retirement planning strategy—that would include other products and investments. An EIA should be positioned as part of the "conservative" money portion of a long-term retirement savings plan.

- *How do you explain the minimum guarantee and how does it relate to the floor?*

The minimum guarantee can be explained as the minimum amount the client will receive *at the end of the index term*. In most contracts, this amount is equal to 90 percent of the original premium, compounded annually at 3 percent. The floor is the minimum amount of indexed interest an annual or multi-year reset contract will earn *in any given year or multiple-year period*—whatever the period may be for calculating and crediting index interest. For most contracts, the floor is 0 percent.

- *How are withdrawals and surrenders handled?*

It is true that most EIAs are not meant for ongoing liquidity needs. Instead, they are designed for accumulation, at least during the initial term. Nevertheless, the majority of EIA contracts do contain withdrawal and surrender provisions, though the consequences of exercising them can be severe. This is one aspect of an EIA that has to be fully explained to a client.

- *What's the death benefit in an EIA?*

Most EIAs provide for the death benefit to be the contract's fully indexed value. This can be quite different from the surrender value.

- *Can the contract continue at the owner's death?*

Since annuity law allows for a spouse to continue a contract, insurers also allow this for their EIAs.

- *Why use an EIA when there are other alternatives, such as variable annuities and mutual funds?*

Again, EIAs are not better—or worse—than variable annuities or mutual funds. They are just different. EIAs are meant for a client's risk-averse dollars, not his or her risk-taking dollars.

- *Can a client ever lose money with an EIA?*

You have to look closely at the product design to answer this question in more than general terms. Certainly, a contract owner's principal is never subject to market risk; principal will never be lost due to downtrends in the market. On the other hand, an early surrender could trigger surrender charges that might invade principal. As far as interest goes, once interest has been credited to a contract's surrender or non-forfeiture values, it too is protected and cannot be lost. However, interest that has not been credited can be lost. This is another example of why it's so important for the practitioner to understand every facet of an EIA contract's provisions.

- *How are withdrawal or surrender charges usually applied?*

EIAs will have either explicit or implicit surrender charges; some have both. Explicit surrender charges are specifically set forth in the contract, usually defined as a percentage of premium deposit or a percentage of account value that is charged against the contract owner in the event he or she withdraws funds or surrenders the contract before the end of the term. An implicit surrender charge is the loss of indexed interest credit due to a withdrawal prior to the end of the term.

- *How does an averaging feature affect an EIA's performance?*

Averaging has its own set of performance characteristics. In a rising market, an EIA with an averaging feature will tend to underperform in comparison to a contract that does not have this feature, but there are many markets in which averaging will out-perform. The important thing to remember is that EIAs are not about market performance. They are about long-term retirement savings, asset allocation and risk management.

- ***Are EIAs covered by state guaranty associations?***

Because they are fixed annuities EIAs are governed, regulated and guaranteed by state governments. They are covered as fixed annuities by state guaranty associations.

- ***What is the alpha, beta and R^2 of an EIA?***

Alpha, beta and R^2 are terms that characterize how well the performance of an investment product correlates to movements in the stock market. They help an investor assess the risk of a particular investment. However, there is a problem with applying these terms to EIAs. The vast majority of EIAs on the market today are fixed annuities. By definition, fixed annuities guarantee principal and are not subject to market risk. Therefore, you should be cautioned against using security terms with nonsecurity products like EIAs.

⬛⬛⬛⬛⬛ **Answer Key to Chapter Review Questions**

CHAPTER 1

1. B
2. D
3. B
4. False
5. False

CHAPTER 2

1. False
2. False
3. B
4. D
5. B
6. B
7. False

CHAPTER 3

1. C
2. False
3. D
4. D
5. B

CHAPTER 4

1. A
2. B
3. D
4. True
5. C
6. A
7. D
8. C

CHAPTER 5

1. C
2. A
3. D
4. D
5. A
6. False
7. B

CHAPTER 6

1. C
2. B
3. False
4. A
5. D

CHAPTER 7

1. C
2. A
3. C
4. B
5. C

CHAPTER 8

1. B
2. C
3. True
4. False

Equity Indexed Annuities
35-Question Multiple-Choice Examination

This exam was designed for those whose firms have selected this course for their firm element continuing education requirement. If the exam is to be graded and tracked by Dearborn, complete the answer sheet at the end of the book, using a black felt-tipped pen, and fax it to Dearborn at 312-836-1939. (To ensure accurate grading, each answer box must be completely filled in.)

If you don't know whether your firm has selected this course or whether Dearborn is to grade the exam, contact your compliance manager.

Note: This exam has not been approved for insurance continuing education and cannot be used for this purpose. If you need insurance continuing education credit for this course, a different exam is required. Contact Dearborn at 1-800-423-4723.

Equity Indexed Annuities

1. An equity indexed annuity can be most accurately described as a

   A. variable annuity
   B. fixed rate annuity
   C. call option
   D. mutual fund

2. EIA Product X is tied to the S&P 500 Index. It marks the index at the point when the contract holder's premium is deposited in the contract and again at the end of the contract's initial term. The difference between the index values at these marks is the methodology behind the interest credited to Product X. Product X is a(n)

   A. annual reset product
   B. low water mark product
   C. digital product
   D. point-to-point product

3. With regard to proper market conduct for EIAs, all of the following are true EXCEPT

   A. the product's traditional fixed annuity features and benefits should be emphasized
   B. the practitioner can explain the trade-offs the products entail in light of the guarantees they provide
   C. only those who hold an NASD license can discuss how an EIA design is or is not credited with dividends
   D. the product should be positioned for "safe money" investing

4. An EIA addresses all of the following investment objectives EXCEPT

   A. safety of principal
   B. guaranteed rate of return
   C. short-term investment horizon
   D. asset management

5. The individual whose life is used to measure the income stream under an annuity contract is the

   A. contract owner
   B. annuitant
   C. beneficiary
   D. none of the above

6. For purposes of calculating index yields for EIA contracts, which of the following dates is used for marking points in time?

   A. Contract holder's birthday
   B. Contract's anniversary date
   C. First day of the first month after the contract is issued
   D. First day of the third month after the contract is issued

7. The choice of investing in a fixed annuity versus a variable annuity usually depends on the

   A. amount of money available for investing
   B. contract holder's investment horizon
   C. contract holder's risk tolerance
   D. contract holder's need for tax-deferral

8. Which of the following is(are) characteristic of both equity indexed annuities and declared-rate fixed annuities?

   A. Death benefit
   B. Minimum guaranteed returns
   C. Both a death benefit and minimum guaranteed returns
   D. Neither a death benefit nor minimum guaranteed returns

9. An equity indexed annuity would most appropriately address which of the following needs?

   A. Tax savings
   B. Short-term liquidity
   C. College funding
   D. Retirement savings

10. The index to which most EIAs link their interest earnings is the

   A. Dow Jones Industrial Average
   B. AMEX
   C. S&P 500
   D. S&P 100

11. The minimum interest rate guaranteed payable on most fixed annuities is

   A. 0 percent
   B. 3 percent
   C. 5 percent
   D. 8 percent

12. Immediate annuities offer

   A. the opportunity to accumulate earnings
   B. a way to methodically distribute income
   C. a means to defer taxation
   D. all of the above

13. An EIA product that contains a cap limits the

   A. amount of premium that can be invested
   B. amount of premium that is linked to the index for interest crediting
   C. amount of index-linked interest that may be credited to the contract
   D. participation rate to less than 100 percent

14. With most declared-rate fixed annuities, the interest rate is declared and payable

   A. annually
   B. monthly
   C. weekly
   D. once, at the contract's inception

15. Assume the S&P 500 Index is 900 on January 1 and on December 31 it is at 1110. What is the S&P 500's yield for that year?

   A. 18.9 percent
   B. 23.3 percent
   C. 32.8 percent
   D. 76.7 percent

16. An EIA product that contains a free withdrawal provision allows the contract holder to withdraw accumulated values without

   A. surrender charge
   B. tax
   C. penalty
   D. any of the above

17. A five-year annual reset EIA has a participation rate of 85 percent and a 20 percent per year vesting schedule. In the first contract year, the S&P 500 yield is determined to be 16 percent. How much of that yield will be credited to the contract's account value?

   A. 3.2 percent
   B. 12.8 percent
   C. 10.88 percent
   D. 13.6 percent

18. Which of the following affects an EIA contract's participation rate?

   A. Prevailing market interest rates
   B. Implied volatility of the market
   C. Both A and B
   D. Neither A nor B

19. A newly purchased EIA contract contains the following features: an 85 percent participation rate, a 16 percent cap and a 0 percent floor. During the first year, the indexed interest yield was determined to be 20 percent. What percentage of that yield will be credited to the contract's account value for that year?

   A. 2.72 percent
   B. 3.4 percent
   C. 16 percent
   D. 17 percent

20. Which of the following EIA products would probably include a floor?

   A. Point-to-point
   B. Low water mark
   C. Annual reset
   D. All of the above

21. All of the following are characteristic of EIAs EXCEPT

   A. provision for a death benefit
   B. surrender charges
   C. annuitization
   D. choice of how premium funds are invested

22. What type of investment does an insurer typically make to provide for an EIA contract's underlying guarantees?

   A. Purchase of bonds
   B. Purchase of call options
   C. Purchase of mutual funds
   D. Purchase of long-term Treasury bills

23. Mark invested $10,000 in a seven-year annual reset EIA. The product has a 90 percent participation rate, a 0 percent floor, an 18 percent cap and a 3 percent minimum guarantee. The first contract year, the S&P 500 yield was a negative 10 percent. How much indexed interest will be credited to Mark's contract that first year?

   A. 0 percent
   B. 2.7 percent
   C. 3 percent
   D. −10 percent

24. The window period of an EIA contract is the point during which

   A. additional premium payments can be made by the contract holder
   B. determination of the participation rate is made
   C. the contract values are fully available
   D. surrender charges are applicable

25. The typical initial term for most EIAs on the market today is

   A. one to three years
   B. three to five years
   C. five to seven years
   D. seven to ten years

26. All of the following statements regarding EIA caps are true EXCEPT

   A. they can be applied annually
   B. they can be applied over the full term of the contract
   C. they are most likely to be used on annual reset products
   D. they cannot be adjusted once set

27. Assume the S&P 500 is at 950 when Earl deposits $10,000 in a seven-year EIA. The contract uses point-to-point interest crediting and provides for 100 percent participation. At the end of the contract's term, the index is at 1550. How much interest will be credited to Earl's contract?

   A. $3,871
   B. $6,316
   C. $10,000
   D. $12,632

28. For purposes of determining the index yield for a high water mark EIA product, the beginning point is the point when the

   A. index values reach their highest point during the contract's term
   B. index values reach their lowest point during the contract's term
   C. premium is deposited in the contract
   D. index values exceed the amount of premium deposited

29. Assume Marie is one year into a seven-year, point-to-point EIA. The contract provides for 95 percent participation and does not contain a vesting schedule. At the end of that first year, the index experienced a 20 percent gain. How much of that gain will be credited to her contract?

   A. 10 percent
   B. 19 percent
   C. 20 percent
   D. This cannot be determined until the end of the seventh year, when the contract matures.

30. All other factors being equal, which of the following EIA product designs usually has the lowest participation rate?

   A. Point-to-point
   B. Low water mark
   C. High water mark
   D. Annual reset

31. What type of investment does an insurer typically make to provide for an EIA contract's index-linked interest?

   A. Purchase of bonds
   B. Purchase of call options
   C. Purchase of mutual funds
   D. Purchase of long-term Treasury bills

32. To the insurer, what is the biggest difference between EIA products and declared-rate fixed annuities?

   A. The investment profile of the individual who purchases these contracts
   B. The investment strategy it must use to manage the products
   C. The manner in which the products' death benefits operate
   D. The assumptions used to predict the products' surrender and withdrawal activities

33. Generally speaking, which of the following consumes the largest portion of an EIA premium dollar?

   A. Covering the contract's indexed-linked interest
   B. Covering the contract's guaranteed values
   C. Covering the administrative costs of issuing the contract
   D. Covering agent commissions

34. For new EIA contract issues, what effect will an increase in interest rates have on participation rates?

   A. They will be lower.
   B. They will be higher.
   C. They will not be affected at all.
   D. They will not be affected unless the contracts include a cap, in which case they will be higher.

35. Generally speaking, in what kind of market will the annual reset design perform the best?

   A. Steadily rising market
   B. Steadily declining market
   C. Volatile market
   D. Stable market

CE Monitored Self-Study Exam
Dearborn Financial Institute, Inc.

Enter your Social Security number

Test ID 00210

| 0 | 7 | 9 | 3 | 1 | 2 | 8 | 4 | 5 | 5 |

Instructions:

1. Fill in each box completely using either a dark marker or black felt-tipped pen. **NO PENCIL!!**
2. FAX the completed sheets to Dearborn at <u>312-836-1939</u>. FAX ONLY the answer sheets.

35Q

PLEASE DO NOT FAX COVER SHEETS OR POST-IT NOTES!
FAX ONLY THIS ANSWER SHEET!
NO PENCIL!

Name

Address

Company / Broker-Dealer

City

State

Zip

Phone #

TEST ANSWERS

	A	B	C	D		A	B	C	D
1	□	□	□	□	18	□	□	□	□
2	□	□	□	□	19	□	□	□	□
3	□	□	□	□	20	□	□	□	□
4	□	□	□	□	21	□	□	□	□
5	□	□	□	□	22	□	□	□	□
6	□	□	□	□	23	□	□	□	□
7	□	□	□	□	24	□	□	□	□
8	□	□	□	□	25	□	□	□	□
9	□	□	□	□	26	□	□	□	□
10	□	□	□	□	27	□	□	□	□
11	□	□	□	□	28	□	□	□	□
12	□	□	□	□	29	□	□	□	□
13	□	□	□	□	30	□	□	□	□
14	□	□	□	□	31	□	□	□	□
15	□	□	□	□	32	□	□	□	□
16	□	□	□	□	33	□	□	□	□
17	□	□	□	□	34	□	□	□	□
					35	□	□	□	□

DEARBORN

EQUITY INDEXED ANNUITIES

- - - - - - - - - - - - - Fold and seal - - - - - - - - - - - - - -

- - - - - - - - - - - - - Fold and seal - - - - - - - - - - - - - -

_____

_____

Dearborn
Financial Institute, Inc.®
ATTN: Tracking Services
155 North Wacker Drive
Chicago, Illinois 60606-1719